"Who would have thought a decade ago that the words inciting shame and outrage would not be slurs identified by a first consonant, or a sexual term with four letters, but the humble pronoun? That's where we are today, and no one could make better sense of this part of speech than our national treasure, John McWhorter. As with all his commentary on language, *Pronoun Trouble* explains its subject with clarity, insight, and good judgment."

—Steven Pinker (he/him/his), author of *The Language Instinct*

"John McWhorter takes a small-seeming subject, the pronoun, one made resonant in the past few years, and with his unique mix of charm, linguistic erudition, and common sense, explains it all to us. Readers may be so taken with his delicate analysis of examples—his passages on 'Ima' and 'let's' are alone worth the price of admission—that they may miss his larger point: we make our languages far more than they make us, and a passionate pluralism of concepts and voices is as essential to a sane view of the way we speak as it is to a sane view of the way we live."

—Adam Gopnik, *The New Yorker*

PRONOUN
TROUBLE

PRONOUN
TROUBLE

The
Story of Us in
Seven Little
Words

JOHN McWHORTER

AVERY
an imprint of Penguin Random House
New York

AVERY

an imprint of Penguin Random House LLC
1745 Broadway, New York, NY 10019
penguinrandomhouse.com

Book design by Daniel Brount

Library of Congress Cataloging-in-Publication Data

Names: McWhorter, John H., author.
Title: Pronoun trouble: the story of us in seven little words / John McWhorter.
Description: New York: Avery, an imprint of Penguin Random House, 2025. |
Identifiers: LCCN 2024030168 (print) | LCCN 2024030169 (ebook) |
ISBN 9780593713280 (hardcover) | ISBN 9780593713297 (epub)
Subjects: LCSH: English language—Pronoun.
Classification: LCC PE1261 .M39 2025 (print) | LCC PE1261 (ebook) |
DDC 425/.55—dc23/eng/20250118
LC record available at https://lccn.loc.gov/2024030168
LC ebook record available at https://lccn.loc.gov/2024030169

Printed in the United States of America
1st Printing

The authorized representative in the EU for product safety and compliance is
Penguin Random House Ireland, Morrison Chambers, 32 Nassau Street,
Dublin D02 YH68, Ireland, https://eu-contact.penguin.ie.

Моей

CONTENTS

PRONOUN
TROUBLE

Introduction

The title of this book is based on a line from one of the cleverest of the Looney Tunes, "Rabbit Seasoning." It is one of the Hunting Trilogy, three shorts of the early 1950s in which Elmer Fudd tries pursuing Bugs Bunny and Daffy Duck only to wind up, between occasional rifle shots at Daffy, essentially spectating as they engage in verbal high jinks. I should mention that getting shot in this cartoon world is a matter not of injury but embarrassment, with the shot leaving Daffy sooty and with his beak out of kilter. But the relevant sequence is:

BUGS: Would you like to shoot me now or wait till you get home?

DAFFY: Shoot him now, shoot him now.

BUGS: You keep out of this; he doesn't have to shoot you now.

DAFFY: Ha! That's it! Hold it right there! Pronoun trouble! It's not "He doesn't have to shoot 'you' now," it's "He doesn't have to shoot 'me' now." Well, I say he does have to shoot me now! So shoot me now!

(BLAM!)

Goofy as Daffy's confusion about the difference between *me* and *you* seems, toddlers take a while to get past a similar mistake. Hearing others refer to themselves with *I* and *my*, and always hearing themselves referred to with *you* and *your*, at first small ones take the pronouns as labels like names. *You* means themselves, and thus they talk about themselves as "you" while referring to another person as "I." One of the cutest things one of my daughters used to say as a toddler was to get someone to pick her up by asking, with such plangent urgency, "Carry you?," repeating what adults had said to her when picking her up. (Her actual enunciation was "Caa-you?" with "aa" being the *a* sound in *cat*.)

As elementary as it seems, the distinction between *me* and

you is a kind of mental gymnastic. It actually makes sense that my daughter heard "Carry-you" as a single word, which she could wield like asking "Water?" Over time, children get that the "you" and "me" parts have to do with the difference between themselves and others, and furthermore that these parts shift rather magically in reference. They must learn that while someone calls themselves "me," you are supposed to refer to them instead as "you," while calling yourself "me," despite that others refer to you as "you."

That's deeper than calling a doggie a doggie. *Me* and *you* require tiny people to learn a trick, as it were, something counterintuitive that they will have to wield moment by moment for their entire lives. Wangling the difference between *me* and *you*, as opposed to just knowing that a giraffe is a giraffe, is a conditioned reflex.

———

This is one of many indications of how deeply pronouns are seated in our linguistic consciousness, crucial to navigating the complexities of human existence and cognition. They are, always and forever, fierce, captious little things, with stories to tell and lessons to teach about what it is to process existence as a human being in an ever-changing world. They are not just "words" in the sense that nouns are. Pronouns, rather, sub for nouns—my partner reminds me that the Russian word for *pronoun* is *mestoimenie*, "in place of name." Pronouns are less words than traffic lights of a kind.

A crucial difference is that a language is always drinking in new nouns, verbs, and adjectives. New nouns are our normal: *iPhone*, *NFT*. New verbs, to someone forty years ago, would include *email*, *text*, and *ping*. To someone from 1950 observing us now, *ginormous* and *cringe* (as in "That's a little cringe, isn't it?") would qualify as new adjectives. But pronouns are not this kind of word, because there are never new ones. Or, as we will explore, attempts to create them rarely get far.

In the same way, there are almost never new prepositions, conjunctions, or articles popping up within our lifetimes. *In*, *but*, and *the* acquire no company; no new words of this kind would flummox the time traveler from 1950. *In*, *but*, and *the* are just directing traffic, shading what we mean when bringing the "real" words into play—*in the house* rather than behind it. To say "But asparagus is better!" means something different than "If asparagus is better!" *The house* is different from *a house*. The "small words" are mortar, not bricks. Roll the dice again and we might not even designate *cat* and *of* with the same term. *Cat* is a "*word* word," while *of* is, well, something else. Pronouns are words of this "else" kind.

Because in European (and many other) languages there tend to be only so many pronouns, comprising a dozen or so words in a little chart, it can be unclear what a heavy workout they get despite their small number. That workout happens for two main reasons. One is that we use pronouns to refer to ourselves (*I*, *me*), and rather obviously, one is given to doing that rather a lot. The other reason is that they function as shorthand for things already spelled out, and shorthand is central to how communication works. We use the whole noun at first, to introduce the concept, but then let the pronoun do the job: "My accountant is pretty fast. He got my taxes done in just a week this year, and he had a lot of other clients."

Illustrating this is something one almost must, when of a certain age, flag while discussing parts of speech: the magnificent *Schoolhouse Rock!* shorts shown on Saturday morning television in the 1970s. I learned nuggets of grammar, numeracy, and history from those gems, too, but do you, whatever age you are, remember the one about pronouns? I did not, until checking while writing this. Lolly and the adverbs, "Conjunction Junction"—those were for the ages, but the pronoun one was a bit of a dud. Useful for us here, though, was its refrain: "'Cause saying all those nouns over and over can really wear you down."

This includes when we address people, where the nouns

are names. We summon Felicia, and talking with her thereafter refer to her as *you*. In much written dialogue, people use each other's names more than they would in real life. In one episode of Lucille Ball's third sitcom, *Here's Lucy*, amid a three-way conversation already established, Lucy says to her friend Vanda, "Well—when did you go on a diet, Vanda?" Unnatural: in real life, for her to use Vanda's name at that point would be an indication of tension: "But that's just the problem, Alice—you never face your demons." In English, mostly, when you talk to someone, you refer to them simply as *you*.

The names of what we discuss, and of who we address, proliferate eternally, but the way we flag them after we have introduced them into a conversation requires just a few little pronouns like *he*, *her*, *you*, and *them*. Between this and the centrality of referring to oneself, these workhorse words become part of our hardwiring. They are among language's nails, screws. We use them as subconsciously as we breathe or walk; they are linguistic basal ganglia.

As such, to mess with our pronouns is to mess with our sense of the order of things, what's up and what's down—life itself. This is especially true with matters controversial, which is why pronouns so often lead to various kinds of agita. All, especially in our times, intuitively get that pronouns have a way of stirring up trouble.

Pronouns indicate gender: *he*, *she*. The two categories can seem fundamental, and thus it may itch when people propose new pronouns that are blank to gender, with *ze* the most influential attempt until the popularity of gender-neutral *they* starting in the late 2010s. This has meant using an old pronoun in a nonbinary way—"Jill got a haircut and now they're waiting for a shampoo"—quite the challenge to many, despite that, at this writing, people under twenty often use it effortlessly.

Pronouns indicate class. This interferes with an eternal attempt to make English better. In the strict sense, there is nothing more logical than the quest to create an explicitly plural form of *you*, to correspond to the relationship between *I* and *we* or *she* and *they*. Normal languages don't have just one word to express the second person regardless of number. Yet all attempts to make English normal and logical in this regard, such as *y'all*, are dismissed as mere slang because they are most used in dialects outside of print and education—i.e., the less classy ones.

Pronouns stand for order, logic. With their often distinct forms called "subject" and "object," they lead one to think that it is sloppy to use the "object" form as the subject of a sentence.

How can you say "Billy and me slept," one is asked, if you wouldn't say "Me slept"? It is never taught that countless languages no one has a problem with do not divide their pronouns into the categories of subject and object in the way we are taught a language must, that even French is one of them, and that in quite a few languages, even saying "Me slept" is perfectly normal. Since we aren't taught these things, it is easy to hear the use of *me* as a "subject" by legions of people as, let's face it, unintelligent.

Pronouns in the hot seat as always. We will examine how these little words have changed over time and dig into the controversies that surround them. Along the way, we will learn things about linguistics in general without it feeling like taking medicine.

——————

It should be noted that I will be straddling a fence throughout. The linguist is taught to describe the way people talk without judgment. We are scientists, not judges or aestheticians; Mendels studying pea plants, not Ruskins assessing the nature of beauty. The commentator, however, has an opinion, offers counsel. Careerwise, I switch-hit between those jobs.

In this book, I will not be able to even pretend impartiality. However, caveat lector: my positions on these matters do not stem from any "conservatism" with which I am sometimes associated (albeit, in terms of sociopolitical leanings, incorrectly). For example, I am a great fan of the new usage of *they*, and think it is a very sad thing that we are taught that it is a form of mental debility to use *me* and other object pronouns as subjects.

But our main goal will be to get a look at this thing called the English pronoun. How we use *they* is just the tip of an iceberg. There is so much good lore, good fun, and good debate in pronouns. Let's dig in.

* 1 *

THE "YOUR HIGHNESS"
OF *I*-NESS

I	we
you	you
he, she, it	they

The reader may reasonably suppose that the hot spot pronoun in this book will be *they*, given the controversies over its usage as singular. However, *I* and *me* are quite full of the dickens if you know where to look. In terms of how they fit into the way English works, *I* and *me* are what one might call a hot mess. It's always all about them.

I . . . Sucks the Air Out of the Room

In fact, if the first-person singular were a musical, it would be called *Leave It to Me!* Except there actually was a musical with that title, and it had little to do with pronouns.* Thus our musical would have to be called *Leave It to I!*

To wit, *I* is always being different. The first-person singular is a-tangle with irregularities, kinks, things you "just have to know," of the kind that make you thankful to have learned the language natively. For example, note:

> They **are** bald cooks, **are**n't they?
> He **is** a bald cook, **is**n't he?
> You **are** a bald cook, **are**n't you?
> I **am** a bald cook, **am**n't I?

Well, it *should* be "amn't," no?

But instead we say "aren't I," which makes no sense. There are places, such as northern England, Scotland, and Ireland,

---

*In 1938, with music by Cole Porter. It was about a diplomatic trip to the Soviet Union (you kind of had to be there). I have a cast album of it in German. Why (1) Germans staged *Leave It to Me!* at all and (2) called it *Vodka Cola* are both unknown to me.

where people use *amn't* in their dialect. "Sure, amn't I never done at the drunken bowsy ever since he left school?" asks a disappointed father in James Joyce's *Dubliners*, where a bowsy is roughly a "little thug," and he's saying that he's always nagging his son. But beyond, *amn't* is conclusively peculiar to the ear—confoundingly so, since it makes such perfect sense.

Aren't I emerged as a mistaken impression. Many centuries ago, *amn't* was as ordinary and widespread as reason would lead us to assume it would have been. But a word like that one is used a lot, and heavily used words and expressions in a language have a way of getting distorted. *Often* becomes "off-en," *probably* becomes "probbly," and *amn't* came to be pronounced "ahnt," which was spelled *an't*.

However, this was across the pond from the United States, where often an *r* after a vowel is written but not pronounced, as in "cah" for *car* and "Pah-kuh" for *Parker*. This can lead to a sense that if a vowel is hanging at the end of a word, there is *always* a missing *r* after it. In American dialects like in some of New England, this is why some people say "sar it" for *saw it*—that sense that if you pronounce *car* as "cah," then the word *saw* must, on some "real" level, be "sar." This is what happened with *an't*—a notion crept in that if you wrote it, it would be "ahrnt." Thus, people started writing it that way—but then seeing this on the page, people actually started saying *aren't*.

Hence, along came *aren't I?*—a mistake, institutionalized in cold print forever. And, as if someone were trying to make this error even more destructive of order, this *aren't* can be used *before* an *I*, but not *after* it. *You aren't, we aren't* are fine, but you can't say *I aren't*—one must just know to say *I'm not* instead.

That's *I* for you. Heavy usage means crazy stuff, and it's why the area around *I* got pretty busted up. This is even more the case with *I* in Black English. Because Black English is nonstandard, its differences from the standard tend to be processed as errors, "bad grammar." But actually, what can seem like mere flouts of rules are often just alternate rules that are more complex than standard English's rather than less.

Black English, for example, can omit the verb *to be* in sentences like "She my sister," "We her friends." However, behold:

They her friends.
We her friends.
She her friend.
You her friend.
I her friend.

Um—not that last one. Even people with no personal relationship to the dialect will possibly sense that there is no such thing as *I her friend*. In Black English, *am* cannot be omitted, at all. Of course no speaker is taught this or thinks about it, but it is as ingrained in a speaker's mind as the masculine gender of *el sombrero* is to a Spanish speaker.

And then there is Black English's magnificent mash-up *Ima*, for "I am going to." The stuffy classical grammarian would term the *Ima* in *Ima tell her tomorrow* as a "first-person singular/future portmanteau," *portmanteau* referring to words that contain two pieces of meaning: here, the *I* part and the part that puts it in the future. Few things better demonstrate what heavy usage does in language than the fact that in *Ima*, the words *going to* have been polished down to a single vowel *a*! However, as always in *I*-land, *Ima* is a one-off, a tricky exception. Take note:

Ima tell her tomorrow.
You-a tell her tomorrow.
He-a tell her tomorrow.

I don't even need to go on—I lost you after the *Ima* one, or should have. After *Ima*, the shortest cut you can take with *going to* is *gon'*: *You gon' tell her tomorrow*. The portmanteau mash-up mainly occurs only in the first-person singular. It's almost as if *Ima* is trying to be a new pronoun. I once saw someone at a linguistics conference presenting an argument that it actually was a pronoun, and while it didn't really go through, I thoroughly understood the impulse.

It becomes almost predictable that if *I* is involved with some aspect of the language, when you give it an inch it takes a yard, with some kind of algal fertility. In England, people in Birmingham refer dismissively to people from the nearby Black Country region as "yam yams." This is in mockery of their dialect having *you am* (pronounced *y'am*) instead of *you are*; more properly, *am* is used in all persons and numbers:

I am	we am
you am	you am
he/she am	they am

It's almost pleasantly counterintuitive from an American perspective. "Everything would be cut and trimmed out and stacked up proper, not like they am now," one speaker was recorded as saying. Of course it has to be *am*, from the first-person singular hotbed, that becomes so monopolistic, setting the terms the way Hollywood does for the film industry.

This usage of *am* even crossed the Atlantic. In Irving Berlin's song "Alexander's Ragtime Band," there is a lyric "That's just the bestest band what am." One usually just lets it pass, but one might wonder just who in the United States has ever actually said "what am" in that way. The answer is black Americans. The Alexander in the lyric is supposed to be a black man, as is clear from flashes of Black English dialect, as well as that the song was a sequel to a previous one about the same Alexander, instantly lost to the ages, whose race was even more explicitly indicated.

Because in the era of minstrel shows and even beyond it, black people were often depicted in ridicule as using *am* beyond the first person, it has been thought that no black person ever actually used it this way, especially as today none do, or even have memories of older heads who did. But many sources of evidence make it clear that in the nineteenth century, this usage of *am* was common among, especially, less educated black people. A neat example is a recording in 1940 of a woman who had been born a slave, recounting a woman many years before on a Sunday morning before church being told "That sure am a pretty dress what you got on!" (Note also the use of *what* similar to the one in "The bestest band what am"!)

Aware of what *I*-ness is like in English overall, we can see that this *am* usage is hardly some peculiar mannerism local to black Americans, but an inheritance of *am* doing its usual in rural England. Brits who uprooted their lives to live in a distant, unfamiliar place were not usually the schooled elites but people of limited learning and resources willing to take chances on migration for the possibility of a better life. They would have included "yam yams" and people of the rural Southwest—and next thing you know, there am a pretty dress in Mississippi!

You am and *they am* seem less odd, in fact, if we know that good old *ain't* started in the first-person singular as well—as the *amn't* we saw earlier. Before *I*, and only there, *amn't* became first *an't* and then *aren't*. But *after* the *I*, *an't* morphed into *ain't*. Because we talk about ourselves a lot, *I ain't* was used quite a bit—it always has to be all about *I*. This made it feel as if *ain't* was *the* way to express not being, rather than just one form among *aren't* and *isn't*. Thus, it jumped the rails to being used with any pronoun instead of just *I*. Hence *you ain't*, *she ain't*, and *we ain't*.

As always, the *I*'s have it, so to speak.

I . . . Is Written Oddly, of Course

It just has to stick out, like someone I knew in college who spent one week in London and came back saying "shedule" for *schedule*. Why is *I*, and only *I*, like that person, just itching to be different, and thus obligatorily capitalized in that way? It serves precisely no purpose.

But it did before printing. In medieval script, a little downward stroke—a graceful chicken scratch, really—was used to write *i*, *m*, *n*, and *u*. An *m*, for example, consisted of three of the little strokes, called *minims*, in a row. Spacing could indicate what letter was meant, but especially with the vagaries of handwriting, ambiguity was inevitable. To make clear that the pronoun *i*—as one wrote it before the capitalizing set in—was intended, two strategies were handy. One was to put a mark over it, which evolved into today's dot on lowercase *i*. The other strategy was to sub in capital *I*, which felt more natural than it would now, as the division of labor we know between lower- and uppercase letters had yet to crystallize. The "capital" letters were thought of more as decorative than as signaling something like the start of a sentence.

It is no accident that the capital *I* sets in first in the north and the Midlands. In Old English, the way to say *I* had been *ic*, which only gradually wore down to just *i*. However, it wore down at different rates from area to area, and the first place this happened was in the north and Midlands. Thus it was there that the capitalization to *I* first settled in, to avoid confusion with the letter *l*, the number one, et cetera. Southward, the word stayed *ic* in many areas as late as the 1500s, and thus capitalization to *I* came later.

I . . . Just Has to Have a Quirky Origin Story

It's one of those things out of place that you don't notice at first.

Pronouns often come in a form used as a subject—*I* ate breakfast—and a form used as an object: He visited *me*. In English, generally, pronouns' object forms are the subject versions with a twist. *He* as the subject, *him* as the object; similarly, *they, them*. Back in the day—way back!—when you were addressing one person, the proper pronoun was not *you*, which was used for addressing two or more people, but *thou*. But only as a subject; the object form was *thee*. The road from subject *she* to object *her* seems crooked until we know that *she* was a sub for the original subject form *heo*—*heo, her*. But what's with *I* and *me*? While *he* and *him* are clearly siblings, *me* seems brought in from somewhere else, like a sibling from Dad's first marriage.

There is a worthy proposal as to why that happens to exemplify the very nature of *I*.

English is a member of the Indo-European family, which includes all but a handful of Europe's languages and quite a few in Iran and points eastward into India. Linguists have

THE "YOUR HIGHNESS" OF *I*-NESS

reconstructed the word for *I* in the single language that would later become today's family of them: roughly, *eg*.

The original language was unwritten, but consensus is ever firmer that it would have been spoken in what is now Ukraine. We will never know what its speakers called it, but the linguistic term for it is the eternally warm and inviting "Proto-Indo-European," or PIE for short.

Words in Indo-European languages for *I* differ so much that it may seem a strain to imagine them starting as *eg*: *I* in English, *je* in French, *yo* in Spanish, *ja* in Russian, *ich* in German, et cetera. But it all makes sense when you know that languages change ooch by ooch. No speaker experiences any major jump in the language in their brief lifetimes, but the creeping never stops, such that what comes out can be staggeringly unlike what went in, just as what was once a tiny shrewesque little bugger skittering in the bushes avoiding dinosaurs is now a giraffe, a capybara, and Vince Vaughn.

What starts as *eg* might become *ek*, and then the vowel changes and it's *ik* (as in Dutch today). And then *ich*. And then just "ee," which then becomes "aye"—as in, *I*! Or it might go differently: *eg* might take on a vowel at the end, as if an Italian immigrant in an old movie were pronouncing it—*ego*. And then people might start accenting it differently—do you send something to someone's ADDress or their addRESS? Or does some Bronze Age villager in Europe call himself EH-go or eh-GO? Because if he prefers the latter, then change still trickles on, such that after a while the "eh" drops off and you have just *go*. Or, as time passes, *yo*, as in Spanish. And since many Spanish speakers pronounce the *y* in *yo* as a *j* sound and say *"jo,"* it won't surprise us that French has its *je*. Or instead, *yo*'s vowel changes to *a* and you get Russian's *ja*.

They're all the same thing but different. But only a closer look suggests how you get from *I* to *me*. Or, actually, from *me* to *I*. *I* must always be different.

Some of the *I* words in ancient Indo-European languages show us what things were like closer to the beginning. Crucial: they are actually longer than little *eg*, with an extra bit on the end.* Sanskrit's is *ahám*. In the language of the foundational text of Zoroastrianism, Persian's great-uncle language Avestan, the word is *azə̄m*. In the Ancient Greek of Homer, the

---

*One linguist (the late Merritt Ruhlen) who favors this origin of *I* bases the argument on a selection of languages broader than Indo-European, from a proposal that Indo-European traces to a mega family called Nostratic that included several other ones. Most language-change specialists beyond Russia consider Nostratic an unprovable notion. I think they are a little too hard on the matter. But I also find the Nostratic data applied to this particular argument too fuzzy to present more widely. I have thus fashioned a more constrained, although also hardly definitive, version of the approach.

word is not the usual *egō* but *egón*. The key here is that they end in *m*. Or in the Greek case, *n*, but *m* and *n* are variations on a sound: there is a reason that the word *seldom* began as *seldan* and *random* began as *randan*.

Here is how this relates to why *I* and *me* look so unalike. Let's take it step by step, linguistics-style:

Step One: These longer *eg*-words in older Indo-European languages seem to be showing that the original state of the word for *I* may have been longer than mere *eg* and was something like *eg-hom*, a form the experts propose. Logically, it makes more sense that a word started long and got shorter through long-term erosion than that it started short and then an extra nubbin just popped on the end for some reason.

Step Two: And just what was this *m* at the end of *eg-hom?* How about if the PIE word for *me* already existed and was, as it happens, *me* (pronounced "may"), and this hanging -*m* was a remnant of this *me* pronoun?

Step Three: But if the -*m* was the part that meant "me," then the question is what the *eg-ho* part had been without the *me*. It seems to have been a decoration that was packed behind *me* so often that a new word was born, like a guest who never moves out, such that we have not only coats but overcoats, shit can also be bullshit, and *fucker* is more often padded out with *mother*.

Step Four: One theory is that the part before -*m* meant "this" or "here," so that *egho-m* meant "This, me" or "Here I am." Latin fans: think of the *eg-ho* as related to the *ec-* in the *ecce* of *ecce homo*, "behold the man." We can't be sure, but it assists in a sense of how this would have worked.

Step Five: But eternally, words get worn away at the edges. Eventually this last bit -*m* wore off, as last bits tend to, and there was just *eg*—which in English became *I*— such that you would never know that *I* is a shortening of a word that meant "This, me!"

"This, me" can seem redundant. But so is a great deal of how language is used in real life. Much of what makes language change is people's desire to be maximally expressive, which tends to entail reinforcement or, put less formally, piling on. This leads to things like *that there* for *that*, or even *irregardless* for *regardless*. "This, me" would be like an arm over one's head and pointing downward at oneself in self-reference.

It wouldn't be as exotic as it may sound for this process to create a new pronoun. Think modern American English, where a fellow might say, pointing to himself: "Who got a raise today? This guy!" Or an utterance I recall from the early 1990s when someone was begging off from joining a party: "This little girl needs to get to sleep early tonight to be fresh for the exam tomorrow." Fiddle with the dials and switches and it isn't that hard to imagine an alternate-universe rainforest English, unpoliced by literacy and writing conventions and allowed to just go its own feckless way, morphing *this guy* into a pronoun *I*. In many languages, such as Hindi, to say *he, she,* and *they* you actually say "that one" and "those ones."

Referring to yourself in the third person need not even be twee and self-promoting. It can be the opposite, a way of referring to yourself at a polite distance to convey humility. Men's version of *I* in Japanese is *boku*. Today it just feels like a masculine, and rather informal, pronoun, but originally it was a whole word that meant "servant." One referred to oneself as "servant" just as one would use "Your Highness" to address a monarch. In Mandarin Chinese, one can refer to oneself as "little person" (*xiǎo rén*) instead of "I" in the same way.

Overall, though, *I*'s origin as "This, me!" would be consistent with the diva essence of this pronoun. Always and forever, *I* makes sure you know it's there.

I . . . Is the Focus of English's Fakest Rule

As the ground zero of exceptions and glitches, *I* and *me* are predictably the focus of English's most mysterious rule: the one that people somehow have trouble mastering despite being native speakers.

I refer to the idea that it is an error to say "Billy and me went to the store." We are taught that the proper rendition is "Billy and I went to the store," because *me* is an object, not subject, form. The smackdown observation is that since you would never say "Me went to the store," certainly you can't say "Billy and me went to the store."

The rule applies to other pronouns as well: we are to say "Billy and he went to the store" rather than *Billy and him*, and so on. But the rule is generally taught in reference to *I* and *me*, with special attention to the problem of *between you and I* instead of *between you and me*. This rule is, in common perception, another matter of *I*-ness.

The rule reminds me of the old *Twilight Zone* episode "Five

THE "YOUR HIGHNESS" OF *I*-NESS

Characters in Search of an Exit," in which a British major, a clown, a hobo, a ballerina, and a bagpiper are caught at the bottom of a mysterious slick-walled tube they can't escape, unable to perceive that they are dolls in a toy-donation barrel.

I understand how utterly logical it seems that pronouns must be used according to whether they are subjects or objects. The problem is that this classification only seems so impregnable within the confines of a straitened perspective on how language works. Pull the camera back, as happens at the end of the *Twilight Zone* episode, and the *Billy and I* rule looks quite different. To wit, the idea of *Billy and me went to the store* as an error is, itself, a misperception, foisted upon endless generations of English speakers.

Exhibit A: Who did it?

For one, English speakers break the "rule" constantly to no comment. If you leave the door open and someone asks "Who left the door open?" your answer is "Me." Never "I." If you answer "I!" it sounds downright off, broken. Note what this means: it is true that while you would never say "Me left the door open," if you answer with a pronoun alone, you do answer those questions with object, not subject, pronouns. This breaks the "rule" we are taught.

You might propose that when you say "Me!" it's short for "It was me!" But note: that leaves us where we started, because in "It was me!" *me* is not an object, either. An object is something acted upon, like the ball kicked or the potato eaten. *I ate the potato* refers to eating an object in both the grammatical as well as literal senses. In "It was me!" the *me* certainly isn't being "was'ed."

> *This is one thing suggesting that in English, pronouns do **not** divide tidily into subjects and objects.*

Exhibit B: I and Billy??

You're supposed to say "Billy and I went to the store," but then if you changed the order and said "I and Billy went to the store," people would look at you funny. But why, if everything is okay as long as you use *I* as a subject? Some might say that it is impolite to put yourself first, but that's an issue of manners rather than grammar, and the problem here is more about the latter. Whether "I and Billy went to the store" sounds pushy (it doesn't to me…), it also sounds, let's face it, *structurally* off-kilter, like something someone new to the language might say. Moreover, if *I and Billy* is brusque, then why do we hear *Me and Billy* as bad grammar, but *not pushy*?

This is more evidence that in English, pronouns do ***not*** *divide tidily into subjects and objects.*

Exhibit C: It is I???

You knock at the door. Asked who's there, you answer, "It is I!"

But you don't. You say "It's me!" despite that *me* in that utterance is certainly not an object. Countless writers of English have been using *me* after the verb *to be* since time immemorial, and there's a reason. To observe the subject/object rule with this phrase sounds so utterly absurd that even the strictest pedants, taking it upon themselves starting in the 1700s to pronounce upon how English should be, tended to make an exception for it, such as pardoning it because *me* was used in expressions like "Woe is me!" way back in Old English. In their sidebar discussions of "It's me," you can sense these stockinged grammar-pusses grappling to square a circle.

Whence the idea that Old English speakers were always right but for some reason speakers of modern English can't quite be trusted?

This is ***yet more*** *evidence that in English, pronouns do* ***not*** *divide tidily into subjects and objects.*

Exhibit D: Why only a few centuries ago?

A final indication that there's something rotten in Denmark on the *Billy and me* issue is the sheer difficulty English speakers have in mastering this supposed rule.

The rub is that in Old English and Middle English, speakers *did* keep their "subject" pronouns and "object" pronouns in the cages we are told they should stay in now. I'll spare you Old English because it might as well be German from our distance, but Middle English, too, never offends the grammar police on the issue of pronouns and cases where *and* is involved. A sentence like "I and my cumpany was arestyd," with *I* used because it is the subject form, was normal (in contrast to today's hopeless "I and Billy were arrested"); another illustrative sentence was "He and I am both of one consanguinity." Only in Modern English did people start "slipping" on the matter.

The crucial question is: Why would English speakers start getting lazy about this supposed rule only in relatively recent years? This was when education and literacy increased rapidly. Old and Middle English were largely oral languages, despite that we encounter them in their written renditions. Think of the characters dragging around in *Monty Python and the Holy Grail* or *The Black Adder*—print was marginal;

for the most part, language was something talked, not written and read. But starting with Modern English, English was a language that increasing proportions of the population could read. In came sniffy grammar guides, exploding in popularity in the 1700s, telling readers how they should put things when using the language themselves, and even scolding writers of yore who had not adhered to these new ideas about what "good" English was. We would expect Anglophones to have become more, rather than less, attendant to grammatical coherence.

But instead, it is in Modern English that the Great Confusion on pronouns as subjects and objects began.* Pedants start calling it out in the 1700s, but this is also when books about "proper" English first began appearing in numbers; almost certainly the "slippage" had become common in the 1600s. Most often it is condemned as suggesting lack of education. "To use the objective instead of the nominative is a *vulgar* error," one scribbler sniffed, meaning with *nominative* what we

---

*The actual history of pronouns' case when used as a subject with *and* has been almost oddly underattended to, with almost all scholars and grammarians for some reason more interested in *It is I* despite that almost nobody has used it in anything like recent memory. The handiest source known to me on the *Billy and me went to the store* topic is the weirdly organized but invaluable Xavier DeKeyser, *Number and Case Relations in 19th Century British English* (Antwerp: Uitgeverij de Nederlandsche Boekhandel, 1975).

call the subject. He continued, "No person of decent education would think of saying, 'Him and me are going to the play.'" Jane Austen put this "vulgar" usage into the mouths of less-educated characters, such as Lucy in *Sense and Sensibility* saying, "My sister and me was often staying with my uncle." But we can know that even educated people were subject to the "confusion," as grammarians of the period complain about that as well. The one above, Parry Gwynne (what else could someone of that name have been but a grammar scold?), condemned educated people for saying "They were coming to see my brother and I," "Let him and I go up and speak to them," and "Between you and I," classifying these as "all faults as heinous as that of the vulgarian who says 'Him and me are going to the play,'—and with less excuse."

The *between you and I* case continues to elicit contempt even today, but that's what happens when a rule is imposed on a language in which it makes no sense.

This particular "mistake" settled in earlier than the *Billy and me* one—as early as Shakespeare we get "All debts are cleared between you and I," as Antonio writes to Bassanio in *The Merchant of Venice*. Shakespeare was not "writing up" and failing.

The question is why.

Was all of this "confusion" the result of some miasma

hanging over the British Isles? And it really would have to be this general, as the "error" happened in nonstandard dialects as well, despite that their usually illiterate Old and Middle English–speaking ancestors had observed the subject/object rule without a thought. In the English of Devon in the southwest until it died out after the 1800s, one could say "Give it to I" as well as "Give it to me." In that Black Country dialect with the *am* fetish, *her* has been constantly used for *she*.

Elsewhere, it's different. Spanish pronouns, for example, do stay on opposite sides of the subject/object fence. I remember noticing on *Sesame Street* as a kid that a segment titled "Me" in English would be titled "Yo" in the Spanish segment, not "Me," Spanish's object form. Thus, for "Billy and I went to the store" the Spanish speaker says "Guillermo y **yo** fuimos a la tienda," and never has to be told not to say "Guillermo y **me** fuimos a la tienda." Is this because of an alertness and diligence native to Spanish across the globe? One imagines the proud bullfighter, with ramrod posture and elegantly cut attire, resolute in using his pronouns properly.

Obviously not, and it returns us to the question as to why some centuries ago there emerged a creeping numbness to grammatical logic among English speakers, hitherto unknown. The Saxon of 600 CE, a Viking once removed, scratching out an existence on the land, battling Danish invaders, besmudged with cookfire smoke, and dying young, keeps *I* and *me* as separate as the kosher cook keeps milk and meat. A millennium-plus later, the hyperliterate Victorian lady trotting about in her starchy clothes, with her proper education and soul-deep concern with propriety, lets *I* and *me* romp in the same yard with nary a care, answering "Me!" when owning that she was the one who did something, and saying "Me and your sister want to give you a present" in her unguarded moments.

Frankly, if we think of inattention to detail, this contrast makes no sense.

> *This is still **more** evidence that in English, pronouns do **not** divide tidily into subjects and objects.*

I ... Was Taught That If You Don't Say "Me Went" ...

Taken together, all of the above leads to a conclusion: there must be a reason other than laziness or mental debility that makes people use *me* as a subject.

Or not.

"Me went"? Out of court.

Over the years I have learned that the observations I just presented tend to make no real impression. People consider it a mic drop riposte that you can't say "Me went to the store."

Some are genially resistant—I recall the friend who just kept saying, "Well, all I know is that my teachers taught that if *I* is the subject, then…" and was quietly but firmly unreachable on the point. Back in the day, when I was a regular writer for *The New Republic*, I did a little piece on the *Billy and me* issue, which they quietly but firmly never published.

Some get angry. The point came up with friends of a friend around 2000, and I am comfortably certain that one-third of the reason I have never heard a thing from any of the friends of the friend in any medium since then despite quite a few nights of party-style evenings is because of that conversation.* Then I will never forget one questioner in an audience for a talk I gave, who was so irate at my dismissal of the rule that I felt like I had insisted that there actually had been weapons

---

*Soren, *your* friends! I know you won't remember any of these party exchanges because you're more at ease with yourself and life than I am and thus don't fetishize what was wrong rather than what was right.

of mass destruction in Iraq. His face had the implacable glare of an eagle.

Which to me means that I need to give one more exhibit, for the first time. Exhibit E.

Exhibit E: Is Latin the model for English?

As we have seen, there are indeed languages that work the way Mr. Eagle Eye thought English does (sorry for that presumption about his argument, but, well... sorry!), where no one has to be reminded to use the pronouns "right." We saw Spanish as an example, and the classicist catches nothing like *Billy and me* in the Latin literature, where the *ego* "I" and the *me* "me" know their places and stay there.

Latin—with Greek, similar in this regard—is the rub here. The idea that a proper language has pronouns used only as subjects and others used only as objects feels so scripturally correct solely because the people who inaugurated the standardization of English thought of Latin and Greek as the quintessence of linguistic eminence. People like Bishop Robert Lowth were steeped in the majestic corpus of Latin and Greek writings, in post-Renaissance thrall to the idea that ancient Greece and Rome were pinnacles of human civilization. To them, English was a country cousin that needed to be exposed to some old paintings and stately music. If Isaac Newton was going to start writing his scientific treatises in English—*Principia Mathematica* in 1687 but *Opticks* in 1704—then English damned well better know how to dress in public!

Thus, one nineteenth-century grammarian condemned people who use *me* as a subject but was relieved that this was largely the uneducated, sniffing, "Had it not been for the general study of the Latin language, it would long since, we suspect, have been the current usage of all classes." Latin, then, was the model for all good language.

But people like this had no way of knowing how a great many other languages worked. Travel was more difficult, and the discipline of linguistics had yet to exist. To the people who set in stone what they thought English should be, as opposed to what it actually was, the "languages of the world" were the ones of Europe and some few Semitic ones of the Middle East like biblical Hebrew, its close relative Aramaic, and the Coptic of ancient Egyptian liturgy, with Persian and Sanskrit thrown in and Chinese perhaps perceived dimly. Europeans were still "exploring" (i.e., exploiting) the world's peoples with little interest in the languages they spoke.

The key point: our sense of "good English" was shaped in the 1700s by people who knew essentially nothing of the languages of Africa, South Asia, Australia, or North and South America. That is, most of the world. What they knew well was Aristotle, Cicero, the Bible, and the Rig Veda.

How an inconvenient number of languages actually work

These days, linguists know how languages work all over the world. There are seven thousand languages, a great many of them have been studied closely, and most of them are so unlike English that it is much of what a college student enjoys about taking a linguistics course. And the idea that a language must corral its pronouns according to whether they are subjects or objects is, from a broader perspective, a tad flat-earther!

This is because so many languages do not work this way. For example, in most of the world, there are languages in which it would be ordinary to say not

I poked him while he slept.

but

I poked him while him slept.

In languages like these, *him*, which we read as the object form, can also be used as the subject. You use the object form when the verb isn't about acting upon something. You don't just poke—you poke *something*. Thus, in a language like this one I am referring to, *He poked*. But with the other verb, *sleep*, you don't sleep something; you just sleep. With verbs that just "hang" like that, in our new friend language, you say *Him slept*.

From a European language perspective, it seems odd that any person would say "Him slept." But languages divide the world and its concepts up in endless ways, and "Him slept" makes a kind of sense if we squint. Poking is something you do to someone, but sleeping is something that happens *to* you. In the same way as you describe other things that happen *to* you like "It rained" or "It hurt," you might just be able to imagine saying "It slept me" instead of "I fell asleep." There are languages in which how you use the "subject" and "object" pronouns expresses that sense of "It slept me."

Let's peek at one of these languages—Kurdish (one dialect of it, actually), related to Persian. A quick note about this language: the verb comes at the end of the sentence rather than in the middle. "I saw him" is this sentence:

Min **ew** dît.

I   him saw.

The object form for *him* is *ew*. Now look at this sentence, where the verb is not one that acts upon something like *see*, but a *sleep*-type one, *go*. You don't go something; you just go. This is how you say "He went":

Ew   çû.
Him went.

The sentence parses as "*Him* went." And this is the only way to say it. There of course is a *he* word, the "subject" pronoun, but you use it only when the verb is the kind that acts upon something.*

For the "subject" form with "sleepy" verbs to be the object form—although often with nouns rather than pronouns—is common in languages beyond Europe and Africa. Readers raised in many of the languages of India, for example, will find the Kurdish sentences less odd than will those raised in English, as Indian languages tend to distinguish "sleepy" subjects and "active" ones in this way in the past tense.

---

*If you really want to know, the *he* word is *wî*, such that "He saw me," with the word order being "He me saw," is *Wî ez dîtim*. I eschewed presenting this in the text because the resemblance of *wî* to English *we* throws a little sand into our eyes.

Of course, English is no more Kurdish than it is Latin. My argument is not that "Him and me went to the store" is okay because that's how you would say it in Kurdish. I am making a more compact point: it is not a bedrock principle of being a language that pronouns always serve either as subjects or objects.

The other kind of language

And so to keep going: suppose another way of being a language is that one pronoun form—say, *me*—is used almost all of the time, except for one form—say, *I*—used in the special situation that it is right next to the verb. That, after all, is the way supposed vulgarians use *I* and *me*. That is what people actually and effortlessly say, just as they do all the other things that make up how English works.

This may sound like special pleading. Okay, there are all of these languages that work like Kurdish, but that doesn't mean that now we can carve out a whole different peculiarity just for English, right? But that's just it: English is no more peculiar in this regard than... French!

The subject pronoun in French is *je*, but the *Billy* sentence is

41

Guillaume et moi sommes allés au magasin.

Moi means "me."

"Guillaume et **je** sommes allés" sounds as absurd in French as answering "They!" in English when pointing to the children who knocked over the lamp. Yet the French have no problem with this, as persnickety as its stewards can be about matters of correctness. Crucially, one would never say "Me went" in French. "I go" in French is "Je vais," never "Moi vais." But after *and*, one uses *moi*, and no one scolds anyone about it.*

At this point we might suppose that French harbors a kink, which English picked up because of proximity. France did rule England for a good while after the Battle of Hastings in 1066, which left several thousand French words in the language, including six just in this sentence. If *Billy and me* seeped into English along with those words, then there could be grounds for deeming it as a mistake.

But that account runs up against two problems.

---

*Indeed, in French the object pronoun is *me*; *moi* is the emphatic one. The point is that one would say neither "Moi vais" nor "Me vais," just as in English we don't say "Me went." Also, indeed the more typical sentence would be "Guillaume et moi, **nous** sommes allés au magasin," where you might say that the subject is *nous* ("we") and therefore, whatever *moi* is, it doesn't matter that it isn't the subject form. But the point is that if you did *not* use *nous*, the proper sentence is still "Guillaume et moi sommes allés au magasin."

First is that people started "confusing" subject and object pronouns in English in the 1600s, centuries after the French reign ended.

Second, French speakers were rather thin on the ground even during the French rule. The French presided but did not overrun England. Isolated words jumped the fence largely through words in print leaking gradually into common language. But the way you put the words together—grammar—doesn't travel as easily. It is more complex and subconsciously controlled than words. Thus, the only way English speakers could have picked up the *Billy and me* practice from French is by hearing French people saying *Billy and me* in their version of English, and then... imitating them! But why would they? "Ah, oui! Monsieur Billee and me went to zee store!"

So it isn't that English picked up a French weirdness. Rather, French and English do their pronouns the same way because of something larger that they have in common. And here is what it is.

How this other kind of language got that way

A major way German is different from its sister language English is that speaking the language requires mastering that endings on the verb change depending on what pronoun you use. English limits this to using the -*s* in the third-person singular, but German has four different endings of this kind. Just sticking to the singular:

	ENGLISH	GERMAN
I	speak	spreche
you	speak	sprichst
he/she/it	speaks	spricht

Spanish is to French as German is to English. French's spelling makes it seem otherwise, and thus I indicate how a verb form is pronounced, in CAPS, rather than the written form. The French verb doesn't change at all in the singular; Spanish's very much does:

	ENGLISH	GERMAN	FRENCH	SPANISH
I	speak	spreche	PARL	hablo
you	speak	sprichst	PARL	hablas
he/she/it	speaks	spricht	PARL	habla

Also, in German the nouns "conjugate," too, so to speak. Articles and adjectives change shape depending on whether the noun coming up is an object, or in the possessive, et cetera, and all of this differs according to whether the noun is masculine, feminine, or neuter. *Der kleine Mann* is "the small man," but you hug *den kleinen Mann*, while if you gave a gift to a small woman it would be to *einer kleinen Frau*—it goes on and on.

We need no more details, but all of these baroque matchings, like special passwords you have to cough up when you want to use a pronoun or article or adjective, are what linguists call *agreement*. The *the* word has to *agree* with the noun in gender, by taking on a certain form: *die* agrees with *Frau* "woman," while *das* agrees with *Boot* "boat." Then you hug not der kleine Mann but den kleinen Mann because our *the* word also has to agree in terms of whether something is a subject or an object. It's the kind of thing that looks hard to an English speaker, requiring tables and charts of things that English largely does without.

And here is the kicker. In some languages, agreement largely wears away—especially if it comes in the form of suffixes, hanging at the end of a word and therefore vulnerable to eroding. When almost all of this kind of *agreement* in a language has fallen off, its speakers start to get numb to the kinds of things it was based on. If your language is no longer reminding you of the difference between, for example, subjects and objects in practically every sentence, then that distinction starts to feel more distant and less urgent.

At a restaurant, the fan of sauvignon blanc is often offered

Sancerre as a substitute. It isn't usually as good, if you ask me, but they're counting on you not being someone who spends their life sampling and contrasting similar wines. If you aren't, then Sancerre will do you fine, and really, you might be hard-pressed to tell it from sauv at all. In terms of stringently cordoning off subject forms from object forms, German and Spanish are sommeliers while English and French buy box wines.*

In a language where agreement has melted away, the new idea may become that there is basically one pronoun for almost everything—*me, moi*—with one on the sidelines used in a single narrow circumstance: English's *I* and French's *je*, despite how primary they seem because of the way we are taught them.†

It is this melting away of agreement, and not plagues of cluelessness, that determines when a language no longer keeps

---

*I'm no wine connoisseur, but *is* Sancerre ever as memorable as a grassy sauvignon blanc? Perhaps it's crude of me to prefer what I believe I've seen referred to as "fruit-forward" flavor.

†French speakers might note that in the spoken language, it is quite common, and almost default, to pair *moi* and *je*, with *je* cast in the shade as an afterthought, as in *"Moi, j'en ai fait deux"* ("Me, I made two"), where there is no especial emphasis intended on the *me*. A sentence like that essentially just means "I made two," with *moi* trying, as it were, to really be the only way to say *I*.

its subject and object pronouns separated on the plate. Differences among the Germanic languages as a group demonstrate this neatly. Germanic includes German, Dutch, Yiddish, Swedish, Norwegian, Danish, Icelandic, and English, and some have a lot more agreement than others.

In German, in which this agreement melting has been relatively slight, "Billy and I went to the store" as "Wilhelm und **mich** gingen in den Laden," rather than "Wilhelm und **ich** gingen," would sound so off you might get a fine. Things are similar in its close relative Dutch, which has less verbal conjugation mess than German but a lot more than English, and, like German, divides nouns into three genders, each with its own agreement variations on articles and adjectives.

But things are different in Danish. Danish takes things much lighter than German, with just two rather than three genders, and verbs with even less agreement in some ways than English, using one form for all three persons in not only the singular, shown here, but the plural as well:

	ENGLISH	GERMAN	FRENCH	SPANISH	DANISH
I	speak	spreche	PARL	hablo	taler
you	speak	sprichst	PARL	hablas	taler
he/she/it	speaks	spricht	PARL	habla	taler

Wouldn't you know: in Danish people can say the equivalent of "Billy and me went to the store." Teachers don't like it; people are reluctant to own up to saying it themselves, et cetera, just as in English. But they do say it.

Now, Danish is one of a trio of languages that can be thought of as dialects of a single one; the other two are Swedish and Norwegian. In those two, people are somewhat less given to saying "Billy and me went..." than in Danish. Overall, Scandinavianness means that you might say "Billy and me went..." but, even in casual speech, you might not. Then English takes it to the next step.

Agreement is even more eroded in English than in the Scandinavian trio, with no gender marking on nouns at all, and our only verbal endings of any kind in any tense being just -*s* and -*ed*. No lists, no tables, no *amo, amas, amat, amamus*. Predictably, English speakers are prone to feeling "Billy and me went to the store" is okay until instructed otherwise.

Back, then, to the idea that a language must use certain pronouns as subjects and certain ones as objects. We would never ask a Kurdish speaker, "Why do you say 'Me slept' when you would never say 'Me poked him'?" Languages can work in different ways. One way is how German works, another is how Kurdish works. English works in yet a different way—the way

French does, where no one says "Me went" but one might say "Me and Billy went," with the world continuing to spin.

Me-ness Envy

The French, with their breezy acceptance of *moi* as subject, have something on us, and we Anglophones need to take a page from them.

If the reason we shouldn't say "Billy and me went to the store" is because we wouldn't say "Me went," then we'd better be ready to include in our contempt the French, quite a few Danes, and, by extension, speakers of languages in which one would say "Me slept," "Me cried," "Me died." In a weird moment, another pedant of the 1800s, one John Mulligan—*that* name sounds like he could have been running a grocery store!—groused that the "uneducated" use *me*

> *whenever they have occasion to use the pronoun of the first person singular in any other way, except as immediately accompanied by the verb to which it serves as subject.*

Mulligan thought he was describing a mistake, but the fact that he could systematize it this way was a clue that he was onto what the actual rule is in English. Roughly, *I* when alone right before the verb; otherwise, *me*.*

I went home.

She paid me.

Billy and me went to the store.

Me and Billy went to the store.

Between you and me.

(Who did it?) Me!

It's me.

Then, *Between you and I* is a hair out of place: as agreement fell away, people of Shakespeare's time started saying it. Today, however, much of its usage is driven by a shorthand sense one internalizes, which is less about subject and object than just thinking, *You have to use* I *after* and*!* Hence, *between you and I.* This is a perfect example of the fact that all languages leak.

Make no mistake: here in the real world, two things are true together. One is that the idea that *me* must always be used

---

*Except when there is an adverb, or parenthetical remark, between the *I* and the verb: "*I actually wore sandals*"; "*I, since it was so hot, wore sandals.*"

as an object does not cohere. The second is that one must pretend otherwise when using language formally.

Intuition and fashion hardly track perfectly with logic. The association of tube socks with aging and tackiness, in favor of little ankle socks, makes not a whit of sense, given how many reasons there are for wanting to protect that lower shin area. But unless one wants to give off a Matlockian air, these days one settles for the ankle socks. (As I write, the fashion is actually reversing at last, which only points up how arbitrary it was in the first place!)

Billy and me is like that. The pox against it is as unnecessary as foot binding, wax beans, and Woody Woodpecker. Yet while we have either expunged or marginalized those, the idea of *Billy and me* as a problem will be as eternal as death and taxes. Whether it makes sense or not, it has been beaten into Anglophones so soundly, with so many of us using the "rule" so effortlessly, that one could consider it to have become less a trembling concession than an actual rule of the language in its way.

Only so many people will ever say "It is I," "fewer people" rather than "less people," or hold their participles from ever dangling and refrain from saying things like "Being the one gastroenterologist in the county, this seemed to be the only way to serve enough people within a short time." But *Billy and*

I can sit so deeply in us that we shoot eagle eyes at he who questions it (I did that on purpose!). *Billy and me*, in a setting where one wants to be taken seriously, sounds to most of us—against reason but implacably—like a belch after a swig of Coors.

Nevertheless, we can restrict *me* to objecthood where called for while also understanding that this restriction is, in the grand scheme of things, as much a fashion as the top hats those pedants wore. The take-home point is that if there had not been a naive fetishization of Latin among educated people a few centuries ago, the idea would never have arisen that English speakers are making a mistake in saying "Me and Henry tried to ski." No one condemns raccoons for not laying eggs, and Latin gives us no more reason to condemn English for using *me* as a subject than to give a bad Yelp review to a Japanese restaurant for not having ketchup and mustard on the table. We just aren't that kind of a language.

Plus, we're busy enough dealing with poor, overstretched little *you*. Not you the reader, of course, but the pronoun.

* 2 *

POOR LITTLE *YOU*

I	we
you	you
he, she, it	they

In English, as it originally was, the pronoun *you* was utterly unlike it is today. More specifically, it was normal.

But What's Normal?

Today we are accustomed to *you* referring to both single people and multiple, cobbling together hacks like *you two, y'all,* and *you guys* if we need to get specific. But other languages have different pronouns for one "you" and two or more "yous." Have you ever noticed that almost no other language you learn has a one-size-fits-all second-person pronoun like *you*?

Yes, in French *vous*, the second-person plural pronoun, can be used in the singular as well. You can say "Comment allez-vous?" to one person as well as two, and you use *vous* with one person as a way of being respectful—the French equivalent of how you use Spanish's *usted* rather than the humble *tú*. But this way of using *vous* is an option, not an absolute. The neutral singular *you* in French is *tu* and is very much alive. In English, *you* is all there is, whether politeness is of issue or not. If we need something more elevated than mere *you* in saying "Do you want to eat now or at eight?," what have we got, *Your Highness*? This seems so familiar to an Anglophone, but in terms of how most languages do things, it is abnormal.

In Old English, *you*, in the proper sense, occupied but a cozy niche in a grander, richer scheme of things. There was a second-person pronoun used for the singular and another one used for the plural. The singular pronoun was *thou*, which also had a different form, *thee*, when used as an object, after prepositions, et cetera, just as *he* now has *him*.

Then *you* was the second-person plural form, but as default as it feels now, at first it was a very specific cog in the machine, used only as the object version like *me*, *him*, and *thee*. The subject version was *ye*. As such, to an Old English speaker, the basic sense was that the second-person pronouns were *thou* and *ye*. This is the *ye* in *hear ye*, which could be translated in modern parlance as "Listen, y'all!"*

It went like this:

	SINGULAR	PLURAL
SUBJECT	thou	ye
OBJECT	thee	you

But there was even more than *thou*, *thee*, *ye*, and *you*. There was a second-person pronoun used when there were,

---

*Incidentally, there was never in English a word *ye* for *the* as in Ye Olde Grog Shoppe. This is based on a misreading of casual handwriting. In Old English, *th* was written with a single letter (called thorn): þ. In rapid writing it was common to let the top of the jug handle peel off a bit, which happened to look like *y*. This made printers start feeling comfortable using *y* for *th*. The shape was recognizable from how thorn came out in handwriting, and printing type was often imported from the Low Countries, whose languages were not written with thorn, and thus had no type for thorn, leaving *y* handy. When thorn fell out of use in England, it was natural to read the *ye* for *the* as "yee," despite that it never had been pronounced that way.

specifically, two people as opposed to three or more: *git*, pronounced "yeet." Then this had its own object form, and one as different from it as *me* is from *I—inc*! That in any version of English *inc* once meant "you two" hardly seems credible today, but it did, including a possessive form *incer*. "Go forth and multiply," an Old English translation of Genesis has it, the directive being to fill the greenly earth with

incre cynne, sunum and dohtrum

Given the context, you likely can glean that *sunum and dohtrum* was "sons and daughters." That *cynne* became *kin*, such that it meant progeny, is not much of a stretch once you get used to the unexpected spelling. But the *incre* is a head-scratcher with no modern descendant: it meant "you two's." *Incre cynne, sunum and dohtrum* was "You two's progeny— sons and daughters." *Incre*, then, brought out that there were exactly two addressees—namely, Adam and Eve.

The second-person pronouns in Old English, then, plotted like this:

	SINGULAR	DUAL	PLURAL
SUBJECT	thou	git	ye
OBJECT	thee	inc	you

Fast-forward to today, when second-person pronouns in English plot like this:

you

What happened?

The Mysterious Eclipse of *Thou*

There's a myth that gets around, that languages always simplify. Beware it, because if this were true, then since human language has existed for possibly two million years and certainly several hundred thousand, all languages would have worn down to one drooling, open-mouthed vowel expressing, roughly, "Hey!" We'd have the communicative abilities of dogs and maybe less.

Thus the reason our modern *you* is so lonely is not that languages are always going Marie Kondo and clearing out all but what is necessary day to day. Here is linguistic reality: under normal conditions, languages both simplify and complexify at the same time, staying more or less at par. For example, here are the equivalents to the pronouns in the previous chart in Latin:

	SINGULAR	PLURAL
SUBJECT	tū	vōs
OBJECT	tē	vōs

Spanish is a continuation of Latin, as in what happened when Latin changed bit by bit over time. Here are those pronouns in Castilian Spanish:

	SINGULAR	FORMAL	PLURAL
SUBJECT	tú	usted	vosotros
OBJECT	te	lo/la	os

If anything, things got more rather than less complicated, because of the emergence of the polite form *usted*, and how you handle it as an object rather than subject. In no version of Spanish has everything worn down to a mere lonely *tú*.

This is normal.

———

As was English, once.

A first thing about French that strikes an Anglophone as odd is that the second-person plural pronoun *vous* can be used to address one person, as in the iconic "Comment allez-vous?" (if one actually uses this now quaintish greeting much!).

But in the grand, or at least European, scheme of things, this use of second-person plural pronouns to address single people has been common for more than a thousand years, including an alternate strategy of having some other pronoun to indicate politeness, such as with *usted* in Spanish (which began as *vuestra merced*, "your mercy"). English today is the odd language of its original continent in lacking a polite pronoun, but English was not always odd. As such, Middle English used *ye* and *you* to address one as well as several people.

The situation was a little more involved than the one familiar today in how French and Spanish are taught, where the polite pronoun is used by all people at first to everyone but children and animals, with the singular pronoun used according to familiarity later. In the Middle Ages, the main factor was not familiarity but status. People of higher status used *thou* downward, to people of lower status, including children and also, alas, men addressing women. People of lower status used *ye* upward, to people of higher status, such that children addressed their parents with *ye* and women did so with their husbands.

It was codified to an extent that can seem almost nasty to us today—one of the challenges of Middle English to an Anglophone time traveler after dealing with the absence of any real medicinal expertise and the blandness of the diet would be mastering how to use second-person pronouns without getting maced over the head. In a letter in 1448, a woman addressed her husband, within all the intimacy of their relationship, as *you*—remember, at this time, this was as if in Spanish a woman were calling her husband *usted*. *Recomaund me* meant "recommend myself" and was a set phrase of salutation; *wete* meant "to know," as in modern *mother wit*:

> *Ryght worshipfull husbond, I recomaund me to **you**, and prey **yow** to wete that on Friday last passed before noon...*

But in a similar letter (of 1621), a loving husband addresses his wife with *thou* forms. The first passage is "Thus in haste entreating thee to be merry..."

> *Thus in hast Intreating **the** to be merry and the more merry to think **thou** hast him in **thy** armes that had rather be with you then in any place vnder heaven; and so I rest **Thy** dear loving husband for ever.*

Shakespeare wrote amid this stage in the *thou/you* alternation. The interplay goes over our heads today. We read or hear the *thou*s as merely archaic and perhaps figure Shake-speare, trapped in the archaic as he was chronologically, just altered between *thou* and *you* randomly. But Othello addresses Iago, who is his ensign, with *thou* while Iago always uses *you* with Othello. This was what would have been expected given their ranks:

OTHELLO
If thou dost love me,
Show me thy thought.

IAGO
My lord, you know I love you.

OTHELLO
I think thou dost;
And for I know thou'rt full of love and honesty
And weigh'st thy words before thou givest them breath.

There was more: people of higher status used mostly *you* with one another regardless of familiarity, and people of lower status used *thou* with one another regardless of familiarity. Cassio is Othello's most loyal general. Despite the affection between them, they are always *you* to each other:

CASSIO

The duke does greet you, General,

And he requires your haste-post-haste appearance,

Even on the instant.

OTHELLO

What is the matter, think you?

Of course because the people using this system were human beings and sociality is nuanced ("dynamic," one might call it today), there was a good deal of play possible within the schema. A switch from *you* to *thou* with the same person conveyed proximity of assorted flavors, be it flirtation, affection, and even disrespect.

Othello is good in showing this as well. Desdemona always addresses Othello as *you*, according to the expected male-female dynamic. And in this scene Othello starts by addressing Desdemona as *you* in return:

OTHELLO

Have you pray'd to-night, Desdemona?

DESDEMONA

Ay, my lord.

OTHELLO

If you bethink yourself of any crime,

Unreconciled as yet to heaven and grace,

Solicit for it straight.

But as things heat up, he addresses her as *thou*:

DESDEMONA

Alas, my lord, what do you mean by that?

OTHELLO

Well, do it and be brief; I will walk by:

I would not kill thy unprepared spirit;

No: heaven forfend! I would not kill thy soul.

His use of *you* at first was irregular, an ominous note. He was conveying frost, distance, and Desdemona, as well as audiences of the time, would have sensed it. His *thou* takes things back to the norm.

Or, in *The Merchant of Venice*, Gobbo uses *thou* with Launcelot once convinced that he is his son:

GOBBO

I cannot think *you* are my son.

LAUNCELOT

I know not what I shall think of that, but I am Launcelot, the Jew's man, and I am sure Margery your wife is
my mother.

GOBBO

Her name is Margery indeed! I'll be sworn if *thou* be
Launcelot, *thou* art mine own flesh and blood.

The toggling between *thou* and *you* conveys a warming
note that the modern language simply cannot with the compact clutch of pronouns that remain to us.

Iceberg Ahead

Based on how the second person works in other European
languages, this is the way things should have stayed.

At least until the twentieth century, when changing stan-
dards of formality would have discouraged the use of singular
you as an affectation and allowed more room for *thou*. This is
what has happened with *tu* over *vous* in French, *du* over *ni* in
Swedish, and many other languages. Learning most Euro-

pean languages includes being taught that while the classic idea is to use formal pronouns with those we know less than intimately, lately the formal pronouns are used less.

As such, the last thing we would expect is that *thou* would no longer exist in standard English. If anything, it should be used more, not less, than *you* in addressing single people. Really—if English were normal, we would be walking around with our flip-flops and iPhones and Drake and whole-grain pasta calling each other *thou*. It would be *you* that felt increasingly antique.

But instead, by the end of the 1600s, *thou* was crouching in a corner, now a note one struck either to connote what we now phrase as "You little..." or to demonstrate pasty, formulaic affection in greetings and farewells. My favorite example is this tirade from a judge interrogating a baker in 1685, where he switches to *thou* forms in striking a menacing tone. One visualizes this from the perspective of the poor man as the judge bends over closer and closer, his irate face full of lines gradually filling the frame as in a Looney Tune directed by Bob Clampett in the 1940s:

> *Now prithee tell me truly, where came Carpenter unto*
> ***you?*** *I must know the Truth of that; remember that I gave*

*you fair Warning, do not tell me a Lye, for I will be sure to treasure up every Lye that **thou** tellest me, and **thou** may'st be certain it will not be for **thy** advantage; I would not terrify **thee** to make **thee** say any thing but the Truth: but assure **thy** self I never met with a lying, sneaking…*

A more temperate example is in a letter by a nun in 1672. In letter after letter, she addresses whomever she is writing to as *you*. But in one to her niece, she uses *thou* forms—but not always, as she would have a century or more before. Rather, she uses *thou* at the opening of the letter when she has a bone to pick with young Gertrude:

*I know not whither I shuld chyd or pitty **thee**, as being ignorant of the cause of **thy** sylence. I am inclyned to fear, **thou** art either sad or sick. The last may excuse **thee**, but the first not at all.*

but then switches to *you* for the body of the letter (*ioyes* are *joys*):

*Keat sais, **you** must make up that trinity of ioyes. But tis time to present the kyndnis of **yr** frinds, lest I want roome.*

and finally closes the letter with *thou* forms in a shower of affection, the written equivalent of a bunch of hugs and pats and kisses and affectionate words said with pursed lips:

> *I am all hys, and **thyne** as much... **thy** most affectionat ante, W.T.*

Only Quakers resisted using *you* to one person out of devotion to equality among people. To them, a formal way of addressing one person seemed inappropriate and even profane. Crucially, however, because among everyone around them *thou* forms were now mostly used in contempt, or to verbally cuddle younger relatives, Quakers often suffered for this usage of *thou* with other people, including violence. Thomas Ellwood, a convert to Quakerism, recounted in 1714 about his father, "I durst not say YOU to him, but THOU or THEE, as the Occasion required, and then would he be sure to fall on me with his Fists." Note what this means: it really was once ordinary in a family that a child called his father *you* but the father called the child *thou*.

One of Quakerism's founders, George Fox, was adamant that singular *you* was even an affront to grammatical logic. As such, he inadvertently illuminated the futility of today's resistance to the use of *they* in the singular ("Each camper knows what they should bring"). Just the title of his book on the matter in 1660 indicated his visceral recoil: *A Battle-Door for Teachers & Professors to Learn Singular & Plural; You to Many and Thou to One; Singular One, Thou; Plural Many, You.*

> *Is he not a Novice and unmannerly, and an Ideot and a Fool, that speaks You to one, which is not to be spoken to a Singular, but to many? O Vulgar Professors and teachers, that speak Plural, when they should Singular. . . . Come you Priests and Professors, have you not learnt your Accidence?*

One can almost see the spittle, but the die was cast. By the 1700s, in standard English *thou* forms were restricted to poetry and religious language, which conserved the Old English–era usage, when *thou* and *ye* really had stayed in their singular/plural lanes regardless of status issues. Hence God being addressed as *thou* in the Bible: *Our father which art in heaven, hallowed be thy name.* But that—even as long ago as when George Washington was a boy—was then, not now.

Some 'Splainin' to Do*

Typically the eclipse of *thou* is simply described as a fact, as if it were nothing out of the ordinary. But in view of other European languages, to merely describe how *you* utterly extinguished *thou* is like a historical chronicle stating:

> *The* Titanic *launched its inaugural voyage from South-ampton, England, on April 10, 1912. It was destined to land in New York City seven days later but never arrived. Woodrow Wilson was elected president in the autumn af-terward, while one of the most purchased recordings of the year was of Harry MacDonough rendering the song "When I Was Twenty-One and You Were Sweet Sixteen."*

No, wait! What sank *thou*?

Second-person pronouns can be sensitive things, no doubt. Addressing someone directly in general, even with a little pronoun, can risk seeming somewhat invasive ("You! Yes, you

---

*I suspect this reference is getting old, but I just had to use it here. This is what Ricky said to Lucy on *I Love Lucy* in the 1950s when upset with her. In his Cuban accent he would say, "Lucy, you got some 'splainin' to do!"

there. You."). In Japanese, one is taught that the word for singular *you* is *anata*, but it's a rookie mistake when English speakers use it as much as we use *you*. Japanese people use a full name or job title, or just leave the pronoun out, as often as not. To use *anata* as often as we use *you* seems either goofy or overbearing, almost the way always using a full name would sound to us. This sensitive spot about *you*-ness is why so many European languages have subbed in the plural pronoun, with its deferent implication that someone is a kind of royalty who embodies more than one soul.

But our question is more specific: Why did *thou* vanish completely?

Because this didn't happen elsewhere, one seeks something specific to English culture but in vain. There is a proposal that *you* triumphed because among the middle classes, the bourgeoisie, it was tricky to decide whether *you* or *thou* was appropriate and the politeness of *you* seemed safer. That may have been true, but the question is why this would have utterly snuffed out, rather than just reined in, *thou*. Middle-classness is hardly an English thing alone. It emerged across Europe. Ibsen's characters, neither rich nor poor; the burgherly sorts in Chekhov's short stories; or the people Arthur Schnitzler depicted in his Vienna in pieces like *La Ronde*—

among all of them, the basic *thou/you* alternation survived: except on the windy island.

Nor can we say the cause was anything about how English grammar works. The collapse of agreement that changed the usage of *I* and *me* and even *thou* and *thee* doesn't apply here. Agreement is one thing, but a difference between singular and plural, so stark and so readily perceptible as part of existence, does not simply flake away like dead skin. One way we know this is that many nonstandard English dialects have retained *thou* to this day. The utter eclipse of *thou* happened in the standard language but scarcely affected the countryside. The usual form in rural dialects is the shortened *tha*, as in *Lady Chatterley's Lover* when Mellors (of Nottinghamshire) says, "Tha mun come ter th' cottage one time" (as in "Thou must come to the cottage one time"). I have more than once been told by people of Yorkshire descent that an olden chastisement for someone who used *thou* (*tha*) with an elder was "Don't thee tha them as thas thee," as in "Don't you 'thou' those who 'thou' you." Another version was "Don't thee thou me—thee thou thissen, and 'ow tha likes thee thouing." *Thissen* is "thou-self," and thus this warning meant "Don't you 'thou' me—you 'thou' yourself, and see how you like your 'thou'-ing."

Meanwhile, in some dialects, the roll of the dice came out

differently—but in essence, the same. In Newfoundland and some Irish English, *you* is used for the singular in the way familiar now, but *ye* is still around, used as the plural of *you*. What's important is that in those dialects, there are still different pronouns for the singular and plural "you." An alternate universe standard English, then, could have kept on using *thou* with one person and *you* with more.

But the loss of agreement suffixes, while not the whole story, was not entirely irrelevant to how English got from six ways of saying *you* to a mere one. In numbing speakers to the difference between subjects and objects, naturally speakers started confusing subject *thou* and object *thee*, as well as subject *ye* and object *you*. In the previous example, the Yorkshire scold has it as "Don't thee thou me" for "Don't you 'thou' me," with *thee* used as the subject instead of the object. Among Quakers, *thee* became the all-purpose pronoun, whether subject or object, edging out *thou* entirely. The first murder trial transcript in America was written in New York City in 1800, trying one Levi Weeks concerning the death of Elma Sands. Some of the key witnesses were Quakers and thus said in their ordinary speech things like "Thee went softly than ever before." This was Quakerism, not archaism, as everyone else in the trial was using only *you*. But beyond Quakers, *thou* and *thee* flickered out and vanished in ordinary speech.

Things had been similar with *ye*. *You*, the object form, had elbowed in and come to usually stand in as both subject and object by the 1500s, with *ye* on the ropes as far back as the late 1400s. Even King Henry VIII wrote in 1528 to Anne Boleyn, about keeping herself in a healthy climate, that "Yow know best what ayre dothe best with yow" rather than "Ye know best." That was as if today, referring to myself, I said "Me knows best what air does me best," except by this time, using *you* in the singular did not feel odd in that way anymore. *Ye* ended up relegated to the same realm of religion and ancientness that *thou* later joined it in.

But there was something larger afoot. The entire realm of the second person in English seems as if it were attacked by a kind of blight, leaving a single ear of corn surviving in what was once a blooming field. For example, *you* was pushed yet further, saddled with *triple* duty, dragged in as the impersonal pronoun: "You end up stuck in the garage if you don't keep that little card."

That seems such a natural way to put it as an Anglophone, but it's a little weird. In Spanish, to say "Here one speaks Spanish" you render it as "Aquí **se habla** español," not "Aquí **tú hablas** español." Never mind what *se* is: for our purposes what matters is that it is neither *I, you, he, she, it, we, they, me, him, her*, or *us*. In the same way, almost all Germanic languages use the word *man* or something similar in this function—"Man muss Deutsch sprechen" ("You have to speak German").

Well into Middle English, English did. When an Old English narration of the John the Baptist episode has it that "They then brought his head in on a plate," it was phrased as "One brought his head in on a plate," drawing attention away from whoever actually did the transporting, as in "His head was brought in." Here, I give you the translation of each word under its Old English one:

Man brohte   þa   his heafod on anum disce.
One brought then his head   on one   plate.

As in, "man" brought then his head on one disc, as in plate. This did not mean "A man brought then his head"—the word for *man* was spelled *mann*. In Old English, *man* was a pronoun only, doing the job *se* now does in Spanish.

In Middle English, this *man* was so well established that just as we often say "ya" instead of *you*, one often said "muh" instead of *man*. To say that if you want to be safe, "Ya shouldn't," you'd say "Me ne auh," as in "Muh no ought." Note: that didn't mean "Me shouldn't" but "Ya shouldn't."

But by the 1400s, this *man*/"muh" pronoun was on the ropes and then gone. Two things filled the gap. In formal language, this was when people started using *one* in this meaning—*One must attend to such things.* That was a mission-creep from a now lost usage of *one* to mean "someone." Archbishop of Canterbury Thomas Cranmer, who colluded with Henry VIII in his quest for authority over the pope, referred in 1537 to "One named Dale, (whom I also knew in Cambridge)." The sentence seems rather ordinary, but we actually wouldn't utter it quite that way: it feels archaic in that we would phrase it as, if not "A guy named Dale," then "*Some*-one named Dale." The step was short between *one* meaning "somebody" to using it in sentences like "One learned to keep quiet," in the meaning of a person of identity unspecified, just "folks"—i.e., somebody.

There are those (ones?) who think that the French had something to do with this new usage of *one*, because they use the pronoun *on* in this same meaning: "Ici on parle français" ("One speaks French here"). Get it? French *on*, English *one*. I officially plead agnostic on that, but highly suspect that it would have happened even if English had been spoken on the southern tip of Chile and had never been in contact with French.

But in the meantime, casual speech—i.e., most of what any language is despite appearances encouraged by the written word—yanked in poor, overworked little *you*: "Ya gotta this, ya better watch out for that."

If you think the reason was that "muh" sounded too much like *me* and confused people, then consider how many meanings *you* stretches across these days, where context takes care of the difference, or if you know German, how many things *sie/Sie* can mean (*she*, *they*, formal *you*), or how far Italian stretches *lei* (both *she* and formal *you*), and let's not even think about what *ci* means in that language.

Homonyms rarely get in a language's way. The peculiar overburdening of *you* was a symptom of something broader about English.

English Ain't Heavy

It started when Old English became Middle English and has never fully stopped: a drive to shed unnecessary baggage, stronger than in most languages. This began when English was imposed on the Celts who lived in Britain originally, followed by Scandinavian invaders who learned English upon settling on the island. Adults don't learn languages as easily or as well as children. This meant that for several centuries before the Norman invasion in 1066, at any given time, for legions of people English was a second language and possibly one they never mastered. This guaranteed that Old English would become less like jangly German, in letting go of marking nouns with meaningless gender and shedding a lot of the endings from verbs and adjectives.

After the Norman invasion, English kept on taking it lighter. But this time it wasn't because of foreigners. The Normans weren't responsible, for example, because as we have seen, there were never enough of them in residence for their rendition of English to become the norm, or even to affect the language significantly. Plus their descendants had all switched to English after about two hundred years, while English continued its quest for the telegraphic for several centuries beyond that.

Germanic languages distinguish *here* from *hither* and *there* from *thither*; English decided not to and rendered the distinction antique.

English uses the reflexive pronoun *self* meaninglessly in a few stray cases like *behave yourself* and *perjure yourself*. *I washed myself* or *I accidentally called myself* is one thing, but if you think about it, when you are behaving yourself, it isn't as if you could behave anyone else! The few examples like that in English are detritus of a cleanup operation, alien to the other Germanic languages, where hundreds of verbs are like *behave yourself* and use *self* to just lend a note of personal internality, such as "remembering oneself" for *remember* and "angering oneself" when getting angry.

Germanic languages almost all have a set of verbs that use *be* instead of *have* in the perfect: Todd *has* worked but now Todd *is* returned, Todd *has* eaten but now Todd *is* flown away. By the 1800s, English retained but a few verbs of this kind— *Arthur is come*—but now essentially has none.

It's as if the language just can't be bothered. The pathway from here:

	SINGULAR	DUAL	PLURAL
SUBJECT	thou	git	ye
OBJECT	thee	inc	you

to here:

you

is part of this larger story, in which English has endlessly side-stepped what it seems to process as the "irritation of nuance," in the terminology of one linguist.*

Just why standard English has found nuance an irritation

---

*Me, I think. *Language Interrupted: Signs of Non-Native Acquisition in Standard Language Grammars* (New York: Oxford University Press, 2007), 59. Not one to bring to the beach, for the record!

in these ways is difficult to glean. According to one school of thought, the reason would be that the cities where English was standardized attracted people from other parts of the country, speaking various dialects of the language. They would have had to adjust to one another to communicate, with a tendency in grammar to favor the basic over the particular, the necessary over the decorative, such that the language got sanded down somewhat.

This is a tempting formulation, especially as the theory involves what are called "high-density versus low-density networks." There is an enticing wonkiness to the terminology. But this kind of dialect mixing was a general feature of urbanization amid the rise of capitalism, no more or less common in London than in Paris, Amsterdam, Stockholm, Florence, Madrid, or Lisbon. It can indeed have a streamlining effect, having likely made Dutch, Danish, Swedish, and Norwegian less grammatically "busy" than German and Icelandic. None of these languages, however, come close to matching what happened to English.

More likely is that English underwent two passes of widespread DIY usage. Before the Normans took over, the Celts and then the Vikings left English in roughly the condition that Dutch, Danish, Swedish, and Norwegian are today. Legions of people learned English as a second language and made it easier. Then we can bring in those cool "low-density net-works." After the Normans—but not because of them—people with different dialects came together in cities and met some-where in the middle, keeping the simplification process going even further. And remember that English dialects get as dif-ferent from one another as *thissen* meaning "yourself" and "You am my friend" as everyday speech. People needed to make adjustments.

In any case, the result was that standard English, as lan-guages go, is rather impoverished in expression of the second person (as well as any number of other distinctions other Ger-manic languages make). Almost any language an Anglophone learns has more ways of saying *you* than English does, not to mention the languages Anglophones *don't* usually learn. To speak English is to make do with occasionally having to stop and specify "just you, not you two," or "You have to clean up after yourself—I don't mean *you*, I mean people in general." *You* is so overdrawn that a natural human impulse is to try to fix the situation.

And yet any attempt to do so is dismissed as slang.

If It *Is* Broke, Fix It?

Wouldn't it make perfect sense for the way to say "you" to two or more people be "yous"?

After all, there are languages worldwide that form their plural pronouns in just that way. In Mandarin, you make things plural by adding the suffix -*men*. This includes with pronouns, where the word for *they* is as if in English we said "hes," and for we, we said "I's"

I	wǒ	WE	wǒmen
YOU	nǐ	Y'ALL	nǐmen
HE/SHE/IT	tā	THEY	tāmen

So, *you* and "yous." That's a closet cleaned out, with compartments, a shoe tree, and a sachet tucked into the back corner.

And in the northeastern United States, a great many people have tried to make sense of *you* with *youse* (with alternate pronunciations such as "yuz" and "yiz"):

I	we
you	youse
he/she/it	they

Smell that dried lavender and cedar filling the air? But no: the people who brought us *youse* have been largely of humble status, and thus it has only attracted ridicule. This is especially rich given that ironically, in the father language that English, German, Swedish, and the other Germanic languages started as, the original word for *you* addressed to two or more people was *yuz*!

Stephen Crane made rich use of *youse* in his *Maggie: A Girl of the Streets* in 1893, depicting very poor whites in the Bowery of New York City. A woman yells, "Come out, all of yehs, come out," while someone else says, "Youse kids makes me tired." *Youse* was likely an import from Ireland: the *Maggie* characters are Irish, and the English of the Irish across the ocean is rich with versions of *youse*. An early example from 1842 is someone writing in "Anglo-Irish" "Who are yiz at all, gintlemin?" James Joyce used it in both letters and his work. One of his letters has "I will send him very gladly if that will make yiz all happy and loving," and a character in his *Dubliners* stories "said *yous* so softly that it passed unnoticed" (in "A Mother"). Even today, one can hear in Belfast "Youse is really stupid" and "I'll phone up youse."

It is often claimed that *youse* emerged when speakers of the Irish language itself, which like any normal language has separate second-person pronouns for singular and plural, wanted their English to do things the way Irish does. But this is like saying that a one-year-old started to walk in imitation of people doing it around her. She would have started walking even if raised by adults who only crawled. It's built in—just as the impulse to have a plural *you* pronoun is.

This is why the American South, and thus also the Black English that was born there, is blessed with *y'all*, and yet it is difficult to think of it neutrally. That is, the very mention of *y'all* almost inevitably elicits, even if internally, a smile, a scowl, a shrug, a sense of proprietorship, or at least something tangier than whatever you feel when thinking about cardboard or gravel.

Y'all is just as swell a hack as *youse*. But alas, it entered American English much later than Old English, first documented in the early 1800s. It likely emerged earlier, as the older writing is, the more formal it tends to be, discouraging the recording of colloquial language. But even if *y'all* was born back in the 1700s, this was during English's standardization, with literacy and schooling ever more widespread. Once a language is in this situation, new developments are seen as departures from "the real language" so tidy and sober in the elegant permanency of writing. Noah Webster would barely tip his hat at *y'all*.

Thus *y'all* has never been accepted as the solution that it is, as opposed to something quaint and maybe a tad ignorant. It certainly doesn't help that it emerged in the South, and as such is also entrenched in Black English. This subjects *y'all* to a double whammy of linguistic discrimination.

Discrimination entails misunderstanding, which has meant that *y'all* has often been dismissed as simply a substitute for *you* in the singular, rather than serving in a plural function. Popular culture is replete with caricatured Southerners using *y'all* to address one person, much to the dismay of many Southerners. In the Looney Tune "Hillbilly Hare," Bugs Bunny meets a pair of hunters, one of whom asks him, "Be y'all a Martin or be y'all a Coy, rabbit?" and later says to him about a lighter, "I think y'all are usin' too strong a fluid!"

But stereotypes have a basis in fact, and the truth is that non-Southerners don't get the idea of singular *y'all* out of nowhere. No one would ask their friend, "So did y'all go get that root canal yet?" But there are subtler cases. A researcher has reported a salesperson asking, "Did y'all find some things to try on?" and later saying, "Just call if y'all need any help with those things." A familiar example is "Y'all come back, ya hear?" said to a single customer who is leaving.

What outsiders miss about these "singular" uses of *y'all* is that they are actually plural. In all of its association with hominess, addressing a single person as *y'all* is a form of the same polite distancing that motivates French using the plural *vous* to address one person, as well as English moving *you* from the plural to the singular in the same way. The salesperson who addresses *you* as *y'all* is tacitly implying that you are with company—given that you very well may have a friend elsewhere in the store or waiting outside—with their addressing you and this hypothetical "them" to step past the directness of addressing just you. Singular *y'all* is, in its way, dainty.

Youse has probably been used to address one person in this same way. In *Maggie: A Girl of the Streets*, Crane has characters saying things like "Ah, youse can't fight, Blue Billie. I kin lick yeh wid' one han'." Crane was going for a kind of anthropological accuracy and thus was not depicting their speech in ridicule. Especially given that Crane did not grow up in poverty and was not even Irish, we must consider that he was making the same mistake many do, of thinking *youse* does the same double duty as *you* rather than filling the plural slot. However, it could also be that "Youse can't fight" implied that the charge was being made not solely at Billie but at his whole crowd, as a way of taking just a bit of the punch out of it.

To be sure, *y'all* is not a *thou* or a *tu*. If you watch someone sit on wet paint, there is no way to even imply that it was you *and* a friend who sat in it. Rare, too, is a family that schedules simultaneous root canals. When someone addresses one person as *y'all*, there is always a ready interpretation of it as plural, even if abstract. *Y'all* is exquisite, the closest an English speaker can get to knowing how it feels to use polite pronouns like *vous* and Russian's *vy* with one person.

Y'all can lend even more intricacy to this English generally so oddly comfortable with leaving things to context. Mandarin's two versions of *we* give us a handy way of getting at the nuance. *Zámen* means "me and you," while *wŏmen* means "me and him/her/them." Thus *zámen* is you and me, but *wŏmen* is me and Michelle, who goes to that school across town. *Wŏmen* extends beyond you and the person you are talking to.

In Southern English, *all y'all*, as opposed to *y'all*, can be used in a similar way. *All y'all* can seem like just an alternate *y'all*, or a way to refer to a big bunch of people. But it can be used Mandarin-style, to distinguish between people you are talking to directly and those people plus a mass of others not present. "Y'all spilled paint on that chair" is one thing, said to two people who then apologize. Saying to a friend, "You hedge fund managers, all y'all ought to do some soul-searching" is another—he is the only hedge fund manager actually present; you are referring to him plus other ones elsewhere. *All y'all* is a way of actually marking that difference in what *you* addressed to more than one person can mean.

The Mandarin kind of *we* is common worldwide, but it is

rare for a language to make that kind of distinction with *you*, between "you all here" and "you all both here and beyond." *All y'all* finally gives English a distinction other languages rarely make! But alas, since language is not just words but sentiments, *y'all* and *all y'all* will likely always summon a sense that a banjo is playing somewhere off-screen. Hardly a bad thing, of course—but generally thought of as okay only when staying "in its place."

True, the line between formal and informal is not as rigorously maintained as it used to be. It is not uncommon to hear people on the radio and podcasts dropping a *y'all* in now and then to sound a friendly note (my sense is this is especially so with black hosts and reporters, but I spend little time in the South, and thus none listening to local Southern radio or podcasts—it may be more race-neutral than I suppose). But it's a note, as *thou* was by the 1600s, "other" rather than neutral. On the grid of standard English pronouns, the middle row will continue to embody a strange continuous stripe across, with *you* covering singular and plural.

To us, a purely plural *you* pronoun accepted as standard language is something we can only imagine at a remove, like what the world outside looks like to insects captured in a jar flapping vainly against the glass. Standard English is the world's only English that bars its speakers from saying, as it were, *y'all*. One of the first items of business in any new variety of English is to ease up the burden on poor *you*. On Pitcairn Island in the Pacific, nine British mutineers from the *Bounty* were stranded in 1790 with eighteen men and women from Tahiti. A new kind of English emerged between them, in which their plural *you* is *y'all-ee*! Caribbean English creole languages have never for a second made do with an all-purpose *you*, in the late 1600s bringing in a pronoun *unu* from the Nigerian language Igbo instead.*

But in standard English, any creative solution elicits chuckles, to the point that some readers may, quite understandably, be missing ones I haven't mentioned, such as the Upper South's *you-uns* and especially Pittsburgh's *yinz*.

And one modern example has even created offense.

---

*Why did all of these languages source that pronoun from a single language out of many? Long story, told in some of my academic work such as in the chapter "Sisters Under the Skin" in *Defining Creole* (New York: Oxford University Press, 2004). Basically, all the Caribbean English creoles began as one creole, which chose this Igbo pronoun once, and then spread across the Caribbean and even to West Africa, where it seeded Sierra Leone's Krio, Nigeria's "Pidgin" (which is a full language, a creole), and other creoles. All of these creole languages have *unu* or a morphing of it, like an inherited mutation in mitochondrial DNA.

"Omigod You Guys!"

That is the title of the opening song in the musical *Legally Blonde*, setting the tone of a story about a flouncy sorority girl who finds a new pathway at Harvard Law School. That lyric sounds *real*, perfectly capturing the way women of that setting actually talk to each other in our times—and a key aspect of that is the *you guys*. I can certainly attest to hearing it constantly used among the female college students I teach.

I can do no better than literature scholar Audrey Bilger in getting across how entrenched *you guys* referring to women now is. She wrote in 2002:

> *Oprah says it. My yoga instructor says it. College students around the country say it. The cast of* Friends *says it, as do my own friends, over and over again. At least 10 to 20 times a day, I hear someone say "you guys" to refer to groups or pairs that include and in some cases consist entirely of women. I get e-mail all the time asking after my (female) partner and me: "How's everything with you guys?" "What are you guys doing for the holidays?" In informal speech and writing, the phrase has become so*

common in American English that it's completely invisible to many who use it.

Bilger didn't like it, and she is not alone. The complaint is that while it may seem handily gender-neutral like the new *they*, it reinforces the idea that maleness is the default. In this, it can even be seen as backward. The days are past when Anglophones were taught by grammarians that *he* refers to both men and women. We have become accustomed to terms such as *flight attendant* rather than *stewardess*. Is it not retrograde to insist that for some reason, *you guys* is a generic reference when it includes the word *guy*, which no one uses alone to refer to women?

A question, though, is why *you guys* is such a holdout. Speakers' effortless use of countless complex grammatical constructions suggests that the use of *me* as a subject is due to something other than slovenliness. In this light we must consider people who would never dream of referring to all humans as *he*, or to someone as a chairwoman, nevertheless casually addressing their own daughters as "you guys." In cases like this, it is useful to consider that there is an alternate explanation.

I respectfully submit one: in *you guys*, *guys* no longer means guys.

I do not intend this as a blasé declaration of the kind musta-chioed grammarians once tossed off about issues like "ge-neric" *he*, which deservedly rankle those who now critique *you guys* addressed to women. Facile pronouncements of that kind lose their street cred given that too many studies have shown—surprise!—that male pronouns used gender-neutrally still make you more likely to think of males.

I mean that in terms of how *you guys* is used—as in, read-ily among even women well attuned to feminist issues—it par-allels a process common in how languages change whether social issues are involved or not. We could argue that the *guys* in *you guys* has gone from being a noun to a piece of gram-mar, just as *going to* has come to mark future tense. When you say "I'm going to figure it out," you do not mean that you will be traveling anywhere; you are in fact not using the word *go-ing* in the sense of motion at all. But it took time for *going to* to start being used in this way. For Chaucer and Shakespeare, *going to* referred to getting somewhere physically; both would have been thrown by someone sitting at a table and saying "I'm going to try to eat all of this in ten minutes" and then fressing down the food but not getting up to go anywhere. *Going to* became a future-tense marker via creeping implication, in that if you are going somewhere to do something, that auto-matically means the action is in the future. But this means that when we use *going to* as a future-tense marker, it is a mere zombie husk of the original words, they having long ago lost their original meaning and become something else en-tirely. We could see the *guys* in *you guys* as the same thing.

Bilger proposed that "calling women guys makes female-ness invisible." That is true if the guys in *you guys* are guys. But when women use it, especially, what if it only looks and sounds like it means "guys," but those using it are expressing just "people"? Here, both maleness and femaleness are invis-ible, because what is meant is sexless.

One thing in support of this interpretation is that *you guys* is not alone in suggesting it. The same women often address one another as *dude*, and, in this, certainly are not addressing one another as men. Rather, *dude* in this usage means simply "human," regardless of the original meaning of the word.

One reading is that the new use of *guys* (as well as *dude*) emerged from a genuine sense of more equality in power with men than before the feminist revolution of the 1970s. Relevant is an exchange in the first *Pitch Perfect* film, in which someone points out that they can see the tuning fork in the pants of the lead, played by Anna Kendrick, and she shoots back, "That's my dick!" The spirit of that line, played more straight than comedic, could be seen as capturing some of the spirit of the female *you guys*.

A legitimate objection would be that *you guys* still sounds like… well, you *guys*, and that this word versus the grammar distinction is therefore cutting the salami a little thin. But a comparison is, of all things, the N-word.

It comes in two flavors: the slur ending in *-er* and the term of endearment ending in *-a*. The latter is deeply entrenched in friendly trash talk among a great many black men as well as others of color, a word meaning "buddy" with a dash of the naughty. It evolved directly from the slur, but it has become, in essence, a new word.

That analysis can seem questionable, in that dictionaries do not have a separate entry for it. However, calls to ban all uses of the N-word typically include the second one, out of the idea that even if it does mean "buddy," it sounds too much like the slur and calls up associations with it. There are two upshots here. First, efforts to stanch the second N-word have been utterly futile; to ask its users to abandon it is like asking people not to chew their food. Second, I suspect that the majority of readers sense a certain clumsiness in a pox on the N-word that includes the term of endearment just "because." A reasonable take is that the two words are *not the same thing*.

You guys submits to a similar analysis. It sounds like what it came from, but has in essence become a homonym of it. The analogy with the N-word extends to its status as a reclamation. Black people fashioned a word intended as a weapon into a compliment. Women calling one another *guys* could be interpreted as related: grabbing *guy* as a statement of power.

Yet there is a residual argument, and a valid one. One might object that it's all well and good for me—a man—to rebottle the old "generic *he*" argument by trotting out some linguistic observations, but the fact remains that no one would ever think of *you gals* as referring to both men and women.

The grimy fact is that the pathway to gender neutrality in language starts from men rather than women.* But the question is to what extent our evaluation of a term should be affected by the unjust parameters that determined the pathway of its development. Just as generic terms tend to begin as male, terms of affection often begin as slurs, such as *n—a*, *bastard, son of a bitch*, or if I may, just once, *bitch* or *dyke*. Yet users of those terms cherish them regardless.

---

*Believe it or not, in the Renaissance era, *child* referred to girls, and only afterward broadened to refer to all children. However, this is only so good an example. *Child* was born in its current meaning, and then for a while narrowed into meaning "girl"—with this driven by a sense of smallness and vulnerability as female.

The reader will note that I write mainly about women saying *you guys* among themselves. Those who are not women may be inclined to consider other choices. One sees calls for *y'all*, but its association with region, race, and slanginess will discourage its universal adoption. Black though I am, starchy "kind of old-school" me would never sound plausible walking into a room and addressing people as *y'all*, women or not, especially if intending a neutral tone. (Imagine me, first class of the semester, near the end: "Okay, y'all, don't forget to look at the syllabus . . ." Not.) More realistic for most will be either *people*—although some find it a little motivational speaker-esque—or *folks*, which happens to be my personal choice. Sometimes, just *all* can work.

————

Casual speech submits ever so reluctantly to control, and I doubt women will stop calling each other *you guys*. This may mean that we are on our way to the enlightened non-woman using terms like *folks*, while among themselves most women use *you guys*, with some men occasionally carping that *you guys* should be okay "because women use it themselves." Any American reader knows what other term occasions exactly that kind of ongoing tension. But that may be the best we can do.

Post Script: But What About Those Middle Pronouns?

	SINGULAR	DUAL	PLURAL
SUBJECT	thou	git	ye
OBJECT	thee	inc	you

Our story has been about *thou*, *thee*, *ye*, and *you* wearing down to *you*, but the reader may want to know what happened to those cool dual pronouns *git* and *inc*.

They were gone after Middle English, and while it would be tidy to ascribe the eclipse to English's irritation at nuance, it would miss a bigger picture.

We can be sure that the language that sired all of today's Germanic languages had dual pronouns, because the first Germanic languages, like Old English, still had them. However, dual pronouns are an exception that proves the rule, in that rather than Modern English being the only Germanic language that lacks them, all the modern Germanic languages do. Across all languages, there is a fragility about dual pronouns: they have a way of not hanging around for long.

Or better, they tend not to hang around in languages that are spoken by large, widespread populations—i.e., dominant ones. In Europe, it is not an accident that the languages that still have dual pronouns are Irish, Slovenian, and a Slavic language even more obscure than Slovenian called Sorbian. All three are spoken by small numbers of people and have not been imposed on large numbers of speakers of other languages. Languages like this tend to retain finer distinctions that their more traveled sister languages let go. It would be much less likely that the three European languages with dual pronouns were Russian, Italian, and Dutch.

A seeming exception is Modern Standard Arabic, spoken quite widely. However, it is an ancient form of Arabic, deliberately kept alive for purposes of religion and cultural unity. Among the great many new Arabic varieties that have developed from it over the past millennium and a half years—like Gulf, Libyan, and Moroccan Arabic—used as everyday spoken language from the Middle East westward to Morocco, dual pronouns have survived in nary a one of them. Arabic's spread meant its introduction to people with other languages, such as the Berber ones in northern Africa. Dual pronouns had little chance under those conditions, with any marking of dualness now panting on the ropes in the modern varieties, only as an ending on a compact number of nouns often encountered in pairs such as hands, eyes, and days (this dual-on-the-ropes will also be familiar to those who know Modern Hebrew).

Thus the dual pronouns in Old English were tokens of the language's emergence as the language of tribes in Denmark and coastal Germany. It isn't that to speak English is to be numb to dualness itself, as the language marks it in quiet ways. *Both* is a dual word: it can't refer to three or more people or things. *Either*, also, is inherently about twoness, compared to *any*, which applies to any number; *neither* is similarly dual compared to *none*. But when it comes to pronouns, these days we have to simply append the number *two*.

* 3 *

WE PERSISTED

I	we
you	you
he, she, it	they

At a fancy dinner, there may be a palate cleanser between two of the heavier courses, something rather miniature and unchallenging. An amuse-bouche, they call it. Two little balls of sorbet, a shot of liqueur, a canapé involving crabmeat and probably chives: an elegant pause.

Among English pronouns, *we* is a couple of sorbet balls—

I'd say apricot brandy is their flavor.* They will be the subject of our amuse-bouche chapter. *We* has never harbored the drama of the other pronouns. It is humble of birth, frugal in its reach, and gives all indication of liking it that way. It is the old-school Yankee farmer as a pronoun.

And yet, like that superannuated stereotype, *we* has some things to teach us if we are inclined to bide-a-wee and listen in. He's—I mean, *we*'s—been around a long time and seen some things.

Why Not Just the Two of Us?

This frugality I mention in *we*—as in, it only spins out so much at a time—is a Middle English thing, one more result of that irritation with nuance. *We* is parsimonious in two ways.

One is that in Old English, there was a distinct pronoun for "we two," *wit*. This paralleled the equivalent dual pronoun for you, *git*. As it happens, *wit* and *git* would seem less odd if we could shake the snow globe again. A language might privilege the cute, quirky dual forms, make them the default, and

---

*I indeed have not experienced apricot brandy–flavored sorbet. But if I did, it would remind me of the character of *we*. Just because.

kick the old general *we* forms to the curb. That is, the vanilla first-person plural pronoun could have become *wit*.

In Icelandic, this is exactly what happened. *We* is *við*, which began as the equivalent of Old English's dual *wit*. This made as much sense as English just bumping the duals instead. Using a pronoun pointing out specifically "we two" is more explicit than trotting out the generic *we*, and communication prioritizes ever brighter ways of putting things as earlier ones lose their punch. There's a short step from two to three, and it is not hard to use a pronoun for just two people to indicate maybe three—why not round up a little? As we have seen, part of language change involves piling on, sometimes at the expense of strict logic, such as the temptation to say "very unique." But from "we two or three," four or more starts to feel plausible. Pretty soon, "we two" just means "we."

We will never know exactly who decided what and when, but we can see ornamentation becoming the default in practically any language. Take Spanish. *We* in French is *nous*, *noi* in Italian, and *nós* in Portuguese. But in Spanish it is *nosotros*, as in *nos otros* "we others." The "others" began as an extra brushstroke—after all, to be part of "we" is inherently to be "other" than somebody. Extra though this was, *nosotros* edged out Spanish's original *nos*. This use of "others" with a plural pronoun is such a natural impulse that it also happened in some French dialects, which is why in Cajun French in Louisiana, *we* is *nous-autes*, "we others."

Nevertheless, in nuance-averse English, the generic *we* edged out the specificity of the dual *wit*. English wants to keep it down-to-earth. But as an illustration of how central chance is to how language changes, one form of English may have taken the Icelandic route: the English that developed on Pitcairn Island when mutineers from the *Bounty* settled there and, isolated from the rest of the world, seeded a new kind of English. With *y'all-ee*, its pronoun peacockery was just getting started.

The Pitcairn English sits in the gray zone between a kind of English and a separate language. For example, the way to say *us* is *uklun*, whose origin has mystified scholars of the language. But perhaps it shouldn't. Just as in Old English *git* had the object form *inc*, *wit*'s object form was *unc*. It had disappeared from writing centuries before the *Bounty* mutiny, but what people continued saying in their ordinary speech for a time is an open question, especially given how many dialects of English there have been, most of them rarely if ever committed to paper. The mutineers who settled on Pitcairn numbered only nine, and it is plausible that at least one of them was still using *unc* and the possessive form *uncer*. If a sense settled in that *uncer* meant not "our" but just "we"—quite possible if only one guy had ever used *unc* and *uncer*—then *uklun* would have been the result of people saying "us ones," except with *uncer*, and therefore at first "uncer ones." This would have been similar to other English dialects such as Appalachian English, where one may say "we-uns."

But getting from *uncer-ones* to *uklun* would have involved a little more. In human language, *r* and *l* are akin, both pronounced with the tongue only partially blocking the breath stream. Try it in your own mouth by comparing how it feels to pronounce a *t* or a *b*, as opposed to an *l* or an *r*. For this reason, the two are easily confused for each other by speakers new to a language that distinguishes both (such as speakers of Japanese for whom *l* can be a challenge to master). Most of the original settlers of Pitcairn were Tahitians rather than native English speakers, and their language lacked both *l* and the English kind of *r* (they had a trill sound, often written as *r*, but actually quite unlike the first sound in *rabbit*). On an island where they played such a large role in how people came to speak natively, they could have heard an English *r* as an English *l*, such that one possible morphing of *uncer ones* would have been... *uklun*.

Is it a coincidence that English once had the dual first-person plural form *unc* and the English of Pitcairn Island has an otherwise utterly inexplicable pronoun *uklun* that means *us*? Coincidence can be dull and surely would be in this case. The fact that people stopped putting *unc* in writing after a certain point is not, in my view, grounds for choosing boredom. After all, you never know what may hold on below the radar in living speech. In talking to a Yiddish speaker about pronouns in that language, I once found to my surprise that in his dialect (a Polish one), plural *you*, when used as an object, is none other than *enk*, just like Old English's *inc*. In that one Yiddish dialect, an antique dual pronoun is still hanging on, although now just marking the ordinary plural. Who knew?

But English's *we* had no use for any of this stringing the dual pronouns along. The duals, vivid or not, had to flake away because one size fits all. And in that same placid, "just the facts" mood, *we* is parsimonious in a second way: leaving us guessing as to just what it even means.

"You-Me-Three-Fellow"?

It's not as basic an issue as it may seem. Rastafarian philosophy refers to *we* as "I and I." This can seem, at first, a ready breakdown of first-person plurality: two "me's." The lesson is wise in reminding us to think of the other person in all of their "I-ness," with their internality as urgent to them as ours is to us. However, it is technically not what *we* means. For a pronoun to have this meaning would stretch empathy beyond what most would regard as natural or even possible.

We means "I plus others." But which others? In chapter 2 we saw how Mandarin makes a distinction between *zámen* meaning "me and you" and *wŏmen* meaning "me and them." This distinction in extent is called *clusivity*, and it's common worldwide. Even English is trying to get some in the second person, with *all y'all* often meaning "you all plus them." In English, *we* evinces no yearning in that direction, but in new languages that put English material to fresh uses, we can see what could have been if the roll of the dice had come out differently.

Tok Pisin is the lingua franca of the eastern half of the island of New Guinea (called Papua New Guinea) and nearby islands. Its story begins with the British colonization of Australia, when a pidgin English lingo emerged between the whites and the local Aboriginals. The Aboriginals spoke dozens of different languages, and the lingo was handy for use between them as well, easier to pick up than any actual language. Versions of this lingo spread castward to the South

Seas and northward to New Guinea, and, used heavily decade after decade, this array of related lingos flowered into actual languages, learned by children. Tok Pisin is one of them.

In the indigenous languages that its creators spoke, one could no more make do with one stolid *we* with its arms crossed than most of us would make do without running water. In those languages, *we*-ness was an umbrella concept for a great many more specific categories. And the people who created Tok Pisin carried this sense of *we*-ness into this new language.

Tok Pisin, therefore, really gets down to cases, distinguishing not only "me and you" versus "me and them," but how many *you*s and *them*s are involved. Thus "me and you two" is "you-me-two-fellow," and so on. *Fellow* comes out in Tok Pisin as *-pela*.

yumi	me and you	*mipela*	me and them
yumitupela	me and you two	*mitupela*	me and those two
yumitripela	me and you three	*mitripela*	me and those three

But here in English, *we* just sits tight. It imitates no other word; instead, it gets imitated.

The original subject pronoun *ye*, for example, *should* be something like *youse*, because the word passed down to the Germanic languages was *yuz*. It is *ye* out of a subconscious rhyming with *we*, because using *we* so often entails being in, or referring to, a group that one may then turn to address as *you*. Or eventually, *ye*. This is also why we say *four* instead of *hore*—*hore* is how the source of our *four* would normally have come out. The Proto-Indo-European word was *kwetwer*, and the *k* sound either stayed the same (Spanish *cuatro*) or changed into a sound like *ch* (Russian has *chetyre*) or *h*, as in Germanic languages (Latin has *canis* but English has *hound*). But *f*??? And just with the word *four*? It's crazy—unless speakers of the father Germanic language started beginning the word with *f* in anticipation of the word for *five*.

Yuz became *ye* because *we* was sitting there *we*-ing.

We shouldn't give *we* too hard a time, though. Languages can be even less precise about the first-person plural—as in, some leave to context whether first or second person is meant. In the Fon language of Togo and Benin in Africa, the only difference between *we* and *y'all* is a tone: *mí* on a high tone for *we* and *mì* on a low tone for *y'all*. Then this language was spoken by many of the slaves brought to the Caribbean, and the new languages they created based on French and English divvied things up the way they were used to. In Haitian Creole, both *we* and *y'all* are *nou*—as in, "we" means both things. This language does not have tone as Fon does, and so context takes care of the difference. It is the same with the word *unu* for *y'all* in some creoles based on English. In the Surinam lingua franca creole Sranan, created mostly by Fon speakers, *unu* can also be used to mean "we"—you can point to yourself and another person and call yourselves, basically, "y'all"!

Give *Us* a Look

Having an object form so different from its subject form—*us* as compared to *we*—may seem to be about all *we* has going on. But just as life in Bedford Falls would have been so different if George Bailey in *It's a Wonderful Life* had never existed, *we*-ness in English has yielded more than just a little word with one change of clothes (or two if you count *ours*). *We* has had a way of injecting the language with shades of meaning fundamental to fully human expression.

Even wallflower *we* has, for example, gifted English, through object form *us*, with the handy little word *let's*.

You have to work to remember that the *'s* began as *us*. We say "Let's eat" and think of it as a short way of saying "Come on, let's eat" with *let's* as a verbal equivalent of the summoning gesture with the arm. But it began as the prim request "Let us" as in "Let us pray."

I can think of no linguistic process more regrettably unknown to the general public than the one that got us from "Let us pray" to "Let's pray." It is when actual words become bits of grammar, which linguists call *grammaticalization*. The term is intimidating, and only comprehensible with a certain amount of familiarity with linguistics. And yet a wider awareness of it would counter the eternal notion that what language change is all about is simplification, which if true would have long left all human languages as verbal equivalents to the drone of Gregorian chants. Rather, languages both simplify and build new material at the same time, and a key way they do the latter is by turning words into things like suffixes.

Let's, then, is not just a matter of two words smashing messily together into one because people talk too fast. As in, it is not, despite what the punctuational tradition of the apostrophe in it suggests, just a salute to an "us" no longer fully pronounced. *Don't* and *do not* have the same meaning. But *let's* and *let us* are different: no Anglophone says "Let us go to McDonald's" except in heavy irony, and even with that, does not process it as meaning "Allow us to go to McDonald's." *Let's* has become its own "word," within which *us* became a mere suffix, whose purpose was no longer to indicate *we*-ness, but to summon people to action. The apostrophe in *let's* is an archaism; ideally it would just be spelled *lets*. *Going to* becoming a future marker is also grammaticalization, and the language long ago nicely "respelled" *going to* as if officializing its grammaticalized (yes, linguists say that) status: *gonna*.

Also, grammaticalization creates prefixes as well as suffixes, and *let's* is an example. In running speech, one might say not "Let's eat another one" but "'Ts-eat another one." To just say *'ts* leaves clarity intact. "'Ts-try a new way," "'Ts-investigate just what that fool did," "'Ts-put in a couple more"—these are ordinary sentences of English. *Let's* has essentially become a little prefix *ts-* that functions to summon people to action— just *ts* from what once was *Let us*.

It's the kind of thing that seems exotic when encountered in another language. In old Russian plays and novels, servants often add a little *-s* to the end of things they say to their employers and other elevated persons. For *yes*, not *da* but *da-s*. For *I'm listening*, not *slušaju* but *slušaju-s*. From English you start to sense that it meant "sir," and indeed, that *-s* was the eroded form of what had begun as *sudar'* for sir, which itself was short for the original word *gosudar'*. *Gosudar'* was a real word; *-s* was a suffix that conveyed respect—a bit of grammar. *Slušaju-s*: "I'm listening, **sire!**" *'Ts-eat another one*: "**I summon us to** eat another one."

There's another neat place that *us* has nosed its way into. At the end of James Joyce's short story "Two Gallants" in *Dubliners*, a guy asks his friend to show him the coin he has managed to get from a maid he is seeing with "Give us a look." Why not "Gimme a look?" Because this usage of *us* is less pushy than using *me*. Implying that the giving will be for the benefit of both of them, even if it won't be, is a softener—a kind of politeness between these outwardly scummyish churls.

This is the same motivation behind someone saying "Let's take our pill" to a child. Imagine it in the voice of Angela Lansbury doing Mrs. Potts in *Beauty and the Beast*—the idea that both you and the sick person are going to take the pill softens what would otherwise be a command to just swallow the goddamned thing. "Let's not get angry" is similar, generally said by someone who themselves is not getting angry. "Don't get angry," in contrast, is usually just asking for it.

In *us*, we have yet another way of addressing a *you* that maintains a deft kind of distance: i.e., politely.

We need things like this, because in comparison to normal European languages with their distinction between *tu* and *vous*, *tú* and *usted*, *du* and *Sie*, *ty* and *vy*, et cetera, English can seem a crude tongue where we once had *thou* and *you* but now only *you* remains, and *sir* is increasingly archaic. (As I write, I am entering the phase of life where people start calling you "sir" and it's hard not to hear it as rendering me a relic for whom the vitalities and sensitivities of youth are now but memories.) There's something to that impression about English. In Japanese, verbs that matter come in different flavors depending on the status of who you're talking to. *Eat* is *taberu* with an acquaintance, *tabemasu* with a colleague, *meshiageru* with a superior, and *itadaku* with your child or a dog. This is equivalent in English to the difference between having some chow, eating, and dining, but must be attended to in Japanese much more diligently (as in, they use their formal word for *eat* more than we use *dine*, a largely ironic word).

It goes further. Depending on who you are and who you are talking to, just *I* can be *uchi*, *atashi*, *watashi*, *ore*, or *boku*. Recall that *boku* started out meaning "servant," and knowing which version of *I* to use is as subtle as understanding why, if you have a bag full of salmon, mackerel, bluefish, and porgies you say "I have a bag full of fish" rather than "I have a bag full of fishes," or that if you read *Atlantic Fishes* you imagine a catalog while if you read *Atlantic Fish* you get hungry. With the American *fish* and the Japanese pronouns, you just have to be there, ideally from childhood.

But English enforces social distance in many ways easy to miss, because the tradition of how it is presented grammatically, in a befogged commitment to making it like Latin, tends to miss the sap of the language. In real English, in each of the three persons, ways of affording a polite remove have been quietly invented.

1) *You.* We avoid saying *you* too directly by using *us.* The Southerner uses *y'all* to address one person, pretending discreetly that there are others present to address. And, in a vernacular vein, these days *sir* is on the ropes and then some, but the way working-class men address men they don't know as "boss" is born from the same strategy as a Frenchman using *vous* with someone they don't know.

2) *I.* We avoid saying *I* too directly by using *us,* depending on our place and dialect. If our place and dialect is the United States and Black English, then a handy way to afford distance is to use two expressions that hardly sound polite. I refer to *a nigga* used by men and *a bitch* used by women.

Bear with me. A black man dwelling in serious, unadulterated Black English, instead of "I haven't eaten today," can say "A nigga hasn't eaten today." This is someone referring to themselves, with the warm intention of this "in-group" version of the N-word, which means "buddy," and it conveys criticism with a touch of sympathy—"Look at me, I don't treat myself right and haven't even fed myself today." As vulgar as it may seem, this usage is based on the same quiet step away that singular *y'all*, Spanish's *usted*, and Japanese's word for *dine* are.

And just as *he* and *she* apply to different genders, this demotically polite first-person singular pronoun in Black English has a feminine form, which is *a bitch*. *A bitch is tired* refers not to a female person other than the speaker, but the speaker herself. The tacit meaning is "Think of me as one of many women or people undergoing this experience, just an ordinary person." Similar is *a bitch is broke*, which conveys that "not only I but many people like me are broke." All of this is about that step away, the discreetness.*

3) *They.* Then finally, the singular *they* that grammarians have so often derided—"A student can hand in their paper at the office until four p.m."—is itself a kind of coded politeness, in

---

*I try not to overlap observations in my books. But as time passes it becomes hard not to make some exceptions, and people who read *Nine Nasty Words* will recall my discussion of these terms. I needed to bring them up again here to illustrate a different facet of them from what I discussed there. And, yes, I'll admit that, also, they're funny.

sidestepping a specification of gender, and thus
keeping the camera lens at a certain distance from
the person referred to.

English described honestly, then, would include politeness
marking in something like this way:

CASUAL	POLITE
I	*us, a nigga, a bitch*
you	*y'all, boss, us*
he/she	singular *they*

Note that pursed-lipped old *we*, in the guise of *us*, pitches
in here twice. *We*, for all of the Rasta "I and I" basic sense we
have of it, is actually a chilly little customer. Psychologist
James Pennebaker notes that *we* in English really means five
things, and warmth is in short supply among them. First is
what we think it is: the pronoun as a hugger: "me and you."
But second is "me and him/her/them," which can be used for
exclusionary purposes. Third is "Let's take our pill," which
heralds unpleasantness, or the waiter's "What will we be having?," which attempts to create a sense of mutuality while also
undercutting any sense we may have had of it. Fourth is the
grand old "royal *we*" as in Queen Victoria's legendary (and
possibly apocryphal) "We are not amused." It is used more

ordinarily to diffuse responsibility, as when Pennebaker notes an administrator said, "We don't feel as though you have completed the forms accurately enough" when in fact only that administrator knew about the forms at all. And then fifth is the political *we*, as in a president's call for what "we" all cherish, where the lack of actual intimacy between the speaker and anyone in the audience promotes only a wan sense of "I and I" or anything close, and becomes a kind of formulaic— and thus coldish—gesture.

We as "Me and Me"?

As to where this staid little pronoun came from, if it evinces any hair out of place, any exuberance, it is that just as the object form of *I* is the unsimilar *me*, the object form of *we* is the alien form *us*. In a tidier system, if *he*'s partner is *him* and *they*'s partner is *them*, *we*'s partner would be something like *wim*.

Why it isn't is lost to history. No line of reasoning links *we* to *us* the way we can guess that *I* started out as "this, me." The Proto-Indo-European *we* was, as it happens, *we* (pronounced "way"), while the word for *us* was *nes*, and nothing about *we* suggests that it started as "these folks, us."

However, while we will likely never know for sure, there is reason to suppose that *us* began as "me's"—as in, *me* marked as a plural, two me's! It's almost too cute, "I and I" among Bronze Age nomads.

One of many ways to tell is that verb conjugation endings tend to stem from the same process that created *let's*, where a pronoun becomes a bit of grammar. The pronouns glom on to the end of a verb and whittle down to a mere suffix, no longer a word on its own, just telling you what person and number we're in. (This is the *agreement* we saw in chapter 1.) This is where Spanish gets:

habl-o	I speak
habl-as	you speak
habl-a	he/she speaks

The suffixes started as whole words.

For example, *carry* in Proto-Indo-European was b^her. We have seen that *I* was ego^h. The order of words differs from language to language, and in this language, the way to say "I carry" would have been to put *I* after *carry* and say "carry-I": $b^her\ ego^h$. Said endlessly for a millennium, $b^her\ ego^h$ could become b^her-o^h, with just a grace note left of what once was ego^h. And *voilà*—Spanish's -*o* ending on *hablo* and verbs beyond.

Knowing this is how things happen sheds some light on the original *us*.

In Spanish, the first-person plural ending is *-mos* (*hablamos*, "we speak").

In French, it is *-ns*: *Allons-y!* "Let's go!"

In Italian, it's *-mo*: *Andiamo!* "Let's go!"

And in Russian, *-m*, in Persian, *-im*, et cetera. Comparing dozens of these endings in Indo-European languages, one can reconstruct that they all started as a pronoun that would have been *mos*, *mes*, *nos*, or *nes*. Close and careful deductions that need not detain us make *mes* a highly plausible contender. And this *mes* (mess? ha!) may very well have been *me's* as in more than one "me"!

Meanwhile *m*'s and *n*'s have a way of changing into each other, and this is why *us* in German is *uns* rather than *ums*. *Uns* is what happens when *mes* becomes *nes*, and then *ns*, and then people start popping a vowel before it: *uns*:

mes > nes > ns > uns

Early on, English dropped that *n*, and thus: *us*. Behold how language changes, kaleidoscopically, yielding the differences between languages that seem so arbitrary but are just business as usual if you know how things happen step by step by step.

———

And now with buttoned-up little *we* having hopefully amused our bouches, *let us* pass on to the second half of our book, where we explore the third-person crew *he*, *she*, and, of course, *they*. Plus *it* for good measure.

* 4 *

S-HE-IT HAPPENS

I	we
you	you
he, she, it	they

In Old English, there was a certain ducks-in-a-row tidiness with the words for *he*, *she*, and *it*. They were all short little words that started with *h*:

HE	*he*
SHE	*heo*
IT	*hit*

You almost want to shoot at them with a little toy gun as they go by on a conveyor belt at a carnival.

Heo for *she* throws us today, but we can think of it as *he* with a feminine ending like *-a* in Spanish: *he-a* like *señorit-a*. It even was likely pronounced roughly "hay-uh."

But if you pulled the camera back, things were almost a little too cute. The word for *they* was weird to our eye and ear as well: *hie*. To our ear it would have sounded too much like the *she* word:

HE	*he*	hay
SHE	*heo*	hay-uh
IT	*hit*	heet
THEY	*hie*	hee-uh

And on top of this, in most of England, the *she* word *heo* was also used to mean *they*. This meant that overall:

HE	*he*	hay
SHE	*heo*	hay-uh
IT	*hit*	heet
THEY	*hie*	hee-uh
ALTERNATE THEY	*heo*	hay-uh

It was worse before it got better: at first in Old English, *heo* had often in many places been pronounced "hee-uh," leaving three different meanings all sounding close to alike:

HE	*he*	hay
SHE	*hio*	hee-uh
IT	*hit*	heet
THEY	*hie*	hee-uh
ALTERNATE THEY	*hio*	hee-uh

Because language is used in context, homonyms are not as much of an obstacle to communication as we may suppose. We have no problem managing that *still* is an adjective meaning immobile—*Writing this book requires my sitting still*—and an adverb referring to continuation—*I am still thinking about those sneakers.* Even amid pronouns, soundalikes can pass unnoticed, such as in German where *she*, *they*, and the polite form of *you* are the same word.*

As such, endless generations of Old English speakers surely managed just fine handling that smudge of "hay-uhs"

---

*I am sometimes corrected on this by people noting that the polite pronoun is spelled with a capital letter, and that when it means "she" the verb takes a different ending than when it means "they" (and "you"). Point taken, but I refer to the simple fact that all three are, in terms of speech, pronounced "zee." A child learning German, not yet literate or thinking about endings, must learn that "zee" can mean all of these things. And does.

and "hee-uhs." But the situation was unideal, to an extent that languages have a way of repairing, at least after a while. Especially when the issue was words used as commonly as pronouns, with such ample opportunity for random creativity and new habits, the Old English situation was unlikely to last forever.

English's Bad "Hay-uh" Day

Old English had, as it were, an issue. *He* and *heo* were too alike. They were so alike that when, almost inevitably, *heo* was often pronounced in rapid speech as just *he*, in some Middle English dialects *he* ended up meaning both *he* and *she*.

Stranger things have happened. Legions of languages worldwide have a single pronoun covering both *he-* and *she-*ness, such as Finnish, Indonesian, Mandarin, and so many others.*

But. Remember the scene in *Jurassic Park* (the first one in the series) where Jeff Goldblum tries to explain chaos theory

---

*In Chinese writing, *he, she,* and *it* are distinguished by distinct variations of one character, yes. But I mean in speech, where all there is is *tā*. A Sinophone baby hears naught but *tā*.

to Laura Dern by showing that a drop of water squirted onto the top of your hand may flow down in any number of directions? (You aren't alone if you don't; no one ever seems to when I bring it up. Wasn't 1993 only about ten minutes ago?) It's a neat demonstration of how language change works. It can be one thing or another, quite randomly.

The sound *oh* might rise up a little, become a little tighter in the lips, and come out as *oo*. That's why two *o*'s together in *food* are pronounced "oo" instead of "oh-oh." The spelling was established when it was pronounced the way it's written: "foh-ohd."

Or: the sound *oh* might move closer to the front of the mouth where you pronounce *eh*, and at that point there's another fork in the road. One thing that could happen is a sound that feels French to us—because it is—where you shape your mouth for *oh* but say *eh*: as in French's *fleur* for *flower*. If you had given someone flowers in Latin, they had been not *fleurs* but *flores*, with the plain *oh* sound.

But another possible outcome is that someone in Philadelphia, where I grew up, says that a store is "cleh-oosed" after ten, where the *oh* in *close* takes on the *eh* sound as an on-ramp. And those aren't the only possibilities for *oh*—it's all about whatever happens to that droplet on Laura Dern's hand, and her hand was a convex plane offering endless possibilities, hardly grooved with just two or three channels like some Badlands landscape. What English did about the *he/heo* problem was determined by this kind of serendipity: structured randomness.

The *he/heo* situation offered myriad possibilities. Some dialects would just allow *he* and *heo* to fall together into *he*, and from then on *he* would mean both *he* and *she*. But even though many languages are okay with that, English had not previously been one of them. To speak English was to distinguish *he* from *she*, and speakers were quietly driven to maintain the distinction.

———

So what did they do? A new word *she* was hardly an inevitable result. There are many places to go from "hay-uh," after all.

One strategy was to work with this *heo* and change its pronunciation to make it something less like *he*. This was what the language most closely related to English—Frisian, spoken in parts of the Netherlands and Germany—chose. One of its *she* pronouns seems distinctly un-English unless you know it is a modern *heo*: *hja* (or in one region, *hju*)—as in "hyah" and "hyoo." There have been English dialects that took that path. You start changing the accent—not "HAY-uh," but "hay-OH," bringing out the *o* in living color. Over time, Jeff Goldblum–style, "hay-OH" drifted into "hay-OO," and then just "HOO."

It's why Yorkshire English has had *hoo* for *she*. In America, and even in most of modern Britain, this can seem so counterintuitive, but genuine old-timey Yorkshire is:

> Hoo's a bit set up now, because hoo thinks I might ha' spoken more civilly; but hoo'll think better on it, and come. I can read her proud bonny face like a book.

Her bonny face—but *hoo* is today's version of old *heo*!

And then in Manchester English, the *h* has worn off, as in the drill Henry Higgins puts Eliza Doolittle through with "hurricanes hardly happen." One might wonder why someone in Manchester of a certain age would say *oo* for *she*, unless you think of a natural progression: *heo* > *hoo* > *oo*.

Getting to *she* was quite a different thing. *She* started as a different word, tapped for a second job.

Spanish classes nouns into two genders, masculine ones that have *el* as *the* and feminine ones that have *la* as *the*. But Old English classed nouns into three:

MASCULINE	FEMININE	NEUTER
se gafol	seo cuppe	þæt fyr
that fork	that cup	that fire

She happened when people started using the feminine *that* word in place of *heo*. In our modern English, largely eschewing labeling things with gender, it can be hard to wrap your head around the idea of *that* having any infusion of gender at all. But if you can wangle the wrapping, the feminine-scented *that*'s suitability as a female pronoun makes sense. It meant roughly what we would mean by "that gal."

After a while, *seo* was no longer used to indicate *that*. English, keeping it light as always, closed down the three-gender business and left everything to the neuter version of *that*, barely changed today from *þæt* (which was pronounced like our *that*, except the *th* was the one we use in *thin* rather than the "soft" one we use in *though*). This also wore down to our modern definite article *the*—Grammaticalization much?— now omnipresent like the Cavendish banana. But *seo* lived on elsewhere—in its new gig as *she*.

There are a couple of movie musicals of the early 1930s where if you look closely you can see that one of the chorus girls was Lucille Ball, hoping to make it in Hollywood in her days before television.* *Seo* in Old English was like Lucy doing time in the chorus. If fate had gone differently, Ball would have given up the business in the 1940s and would be a footnote today, just as *seo* could have just disappeared as a word for *that* and never been known again except to specialists. But as it happened, Ball landed the lead in a radio sitcom that became a hit and evolved into *I Love Lucy*, and *seo* landed a lead role as a feminine subject pronoun and became a *she*. (Of course, these two things were causally related!)

At this point there were three outcomes possible. Only one of them was our *she*, and that took some steps.

First, *seo* "SAY-oh" did the same accent shift as *heo* and became "shay-OH."

Second, "shay-OH" shortened to just *scho*, pronounced "show."

Third, the same vowel change that led *food* from being pronounced "fode" to "fude" made *scho* into *shoo*.

Fourth was getting *shoo* to *she*.

There was a standing temptation for that last step to

Roman Scandals and *Kid Millions*. And there's another early talkie musical where if you look really closely you can see that one of the chorus girls was Vivian Vance, a gig unremarked in any biographical source on her. The film is *Take a Chance*, during the "Eadie Was a Lady" number.

129

happen, with *shoo* being in a pair with *he*. Words in that kind of relationship have a way of becoming more alike than they once were, like married couples. We have seen how *hore* became *four* and *yuz* became *ye*. Because of things like that, you can "just know" that *he* and *shoo* may one day become *he* and *she*.* And that was step four.

But *she* was just one possible end point. Just as there is no reason to think of humans as the inevitable pinnacle of evolution, there is nothing default about *she*. There was no problem with stopping, for example, at *scho*. Today in the northerly Shetland and Orkney Islands above Scotland, the word remains *sho*. No *shoo*, no *she*—they like it the way it was a thousand years ago, thank you very much.

And then there is the third possible outcome, where it gets to *shoo* but stops there. In County Wexford in Ireland, into the 1800s there was a dialect of English spoken called Yola, which had been transported there in the 1100s and had thrived since then, going its own way apart from British English. By the 1800s, it had remained more like Middle English than any British English, and *she* was still *shoo*. There were people alive

---

*And yes, the *she* can be the model, too: in places, *hoo* and *shoo* have emerged from a different roll of the dice. I refer to Frisian's usual *she* pronoun these days, which is pronounced roughly "soo," with *he* being roughly "hoo."

during the reign of Queen Victoria who said "Thaar shoo goeth" for "There she goes."

The only reason *she* seems like the default outcome is that it happened to be the form in what happened to become standard English. However, in the grander scheme of things, *she* was but one of many rolls of the dice:

Antiquity	Modern
heo (Old English) > *hoo* (Yorkshire) > *oo* (Manchester)	
seo (Old English) > *sho* (Shetlands) > *shoo* (Yola) > *she* (standard)	

If the English of the Shetland Islands had been the variety embraced and cultivated as the standard, textbooks would note that down in the south, *sho* "underwent a most interesting transformation first to *shoo*, and then, influenced by *he*, to *shee*." Old books and plays would depict the churlish old peasants with their quaint *shee* instead of proper *sho*.

It would be a tad irresponsible not to at least mention an alternate version of the *she* story, with *heo* becoming *she* by stepwise transformation and *seo* not even involved. You start with *hyoh*. Then the *hy-* part takes on a hissing quality, which ultimately focused into a *sh* sound. *Voilà*—another pathway to *scho*. This strikes me as clever but forced. A *hy* just might become a *sh*, but then a bird just might evolve to become twelve feet tall. There were moas indeed, but 'tis a stretch, in both senses. There is, to me at least, an "I was saying Boo-urns" quality to the "hissing *heo*" story that should be avoided unless necessary.*

In any case, all of this is why *she* and *her* don't match the way *he* and *him* do. It's *she* that is the odd one out, as *heo* and *her* made a nice little pair. It's also why it doesn't work the other way around, with *he/him* and *she/shim*.

Once established, *she* has not kept her head down, which is clear if you listen for the less official usages of the language, where English can take its natural courses. For example, even though *me* is indeed used as a subject in normal English ("Who did that?" "Me.") no one goes as far as allowing it in the sacred position of right before the verb. "Me did it" is hopeless no matter how colloquial one is. Call me permissive, but I would never pretend anyone ever says "Me did it," or uses

---

*I refer to the *Simpsons* episode "A Star Is Burns," in which a crowd boos Mr. Burns and he wonders whether just perhaps they had been cheering him with "Boo-urns!" The crowd boos again, after which mealy old Hans Moleman croaks, "I was saying Boo-urns." I believe that is my favorite line of the entire series (but I largely let it go, as I sense many did, after about season 12).

her in a sentence like "Her is a kinda doll what drives a fella bats."

That, for example, is a line in a comedy song called "Her Is" in the musical *The Pajama Game*, and part of the joke is that "her is" is an exaggeration of how this 1950s white working-man character would talk. But! It wouldn't seem as funny across the Atlantic in the Black Country dialect around Birmingham, where people do use *her* right before the verb: "Her used to go every day." "He told me her was coming." "Her's all right."

She is even part of a salute to English's days of meaningless gender. Always, *she* has held on when referring to certain vehicles such as cars and ships (and some large animals such as whales with "Thar she blows!," although the idea would have been that whales are so large as to seem like vehicles). But with some younger folk, this use of *she* has moved to a wider range of things.

Some real-life examples include "I've got some tea to spill, and she's hot," with the tea in question being not the beverage but gossip. Or, one woman shows another a photo and asks, "What do you think of my dress?" and her friend's assessment is "She's giving me old-lady vibes." The take on a burrito might be "Whoa, she's spicy!" or "She's not playing!" A steep hill can be a *she*: "Watch out, she's steep!"

Why are gossip, a dress, a hill, and a burrito "she"? This has its roots in gay slang, where it was common especially in earlier generations for gay men to refer to one another as "she." While this usage could take on various shadings, it was primarily a marker of in-group membership, indicating that one was, as it were, one of the "boys in the band." It would seem that the affection conveyed by referring to a fellow gay man as "she" has extended from personhood to objecthood. Gossip referred to as "she" is something one loves and anticipates fondly, gossip being a fundamental aspect of social bonding. Calling someone's dress you don't adore "she" blunts the sting of just calling the dress fugly* instead. The burrito and the hill become *she*'s as a sign of admiration of the challenge they present.

One evolution of *motherfucker* has been similar in terms of meaning. It starts as an epithet. Then it dilutes into a way of saying "ordinary person": "There were so many motherfuckers in there I could barely move my arms!" It then becomes an affectionate way of referring to a thing. At this late stage in the game, because long-term usage tends to wear words down and in addition one might wish to euphemize, the proper expres-

---

*Fucking ugly (of course I am quoting "the kids").

sion here is *mother*. In 1986, in the comic strip *Bloom County*, Opus the penguin and Steve Dallas occasionally played in a rock band. In one episode, Opus proposed a couple of subtle musical effects in a song, and Dallas grunted, "Just wing that mother." Music as "mother" is music you feel as true and fine; the gossip as "she" is similar.

The new "she," as I write, is most used by gay men but has jumped the fence to many young folk in general. As gay-positivity edges ever closer to the default among the young, one suspects "she" (see, I'm awkwardly trying to use it) will dig in further. If English were truly left alone, spoken apart from any kind of print, education, social stratification, or judgment, a possible pathway would be that over time the tacit affection in this usage of *she* would dilute, and it would become regular that certain things and concepts were referred to as "she" for no reason any speaker could any longer explain.

For now, it's just fun to hear.

He the People

One of many reasons the "hissing *heo*" account falls short is that it is more expected that pronouns start as words meaning *that* and *this* and *the*. *Seo* becoming *she* only recapitulated the way *he* had been born: the original Proto-Indo-European word meant "this."

Even now we can refer to someone as "this one" rather than *he*. It's just that for us, "this one" can have a narrower meaning than *he*. Using it to refer to a person can convey a quietly dismissive intent. An alternative is "that one," so unfortunately used by Senator John McCain in a presidential debate with Barack Obama in 2008. The air of objectification and distancing was a sadly graceless moment for McCain, but in the formal sense it highlighted the essence of third-person pronouns: to single someone or something out.

There is nothing primordial or "old" about a language using *this* and *that* to mean *he* (and *she*). It passed into early Indo-European languages like Sanskrit and the Old Persian that King Darius had so majestically carved onto Mount Behistun in Iran, and today *that* is still used for *he* and *she* in Hindi, Urdu, and languages related to them in India. Third-person pronouns are the same as *that* or *this* in Basque and Turkish, too, as well as countless languages little known beyond their homelands.

And under that impulse, English continues to ever bubble up ways of altering *he* and *she* to sound thinglike, as if seeking the original state. Common is doing this as a way of conveying attitude beyond the neutral. "Here comes his nibs," for example, has implied that the person thinks of himself as a big deal, for reasons perhaps shaky; "His nibs will have his tea now," you might say about your uncle with a certain pluckiness of ego whose source is not entirely clear. It has also been used with *her*. There was an album in the 1950s by a pop singer named Georgia Gibbs called "Her Nibs, Georgia Gibbs," conveying "The great Georgia Gibbs!" You can't help wondering where *nibs* (sometimes it has been *nabs*) came from, and the proposals are all such a mess that I suspect we will never know. It presumably began in Britain, but the fact that American buyers were expected to know the expression in 1958 shows that it made the crossing, although I have never heard it used live in my lifetime.

He has not been as much of a shape-shifter through time as *she*, but like any word, it has hardly stayed the same in all places. Of course in rapid speech it tends to come out as *'e*, a lone single vowel. That vowel might loosen up into a mere *ah*, and in places, it has. And not just places known to few—the English Shakespeare lived in included dialects in which *he* was "ah," which he wrote as *a'*. This is so weird and opaque to us today that it's the kind of thing that Shakespeare directors tend to quietly modernize, but what Claudio originally says in *Much Ado About Nothing* is:

If he be not in love with some woman, there is no
believing old signs: a' brushes his hat o'
mornings; what should that bode?

In *All's Well That Ends Well*, Parolles says, "A' was a botch-
er's 'prentice in Paris." Antony in *Antony and Cleopatra*
asks, "Cried he? and begg'd a' pardon?"—meaning "begged *he*
pardon?"

This *ah* was the next step that *he* "wanted" to take in England, and as unfamiliar as it seems, it traveled incognito to
the New World. Today, there are Jamaicans using *a'* in ceremonies communing with their ancestors. Why?

It started with speakers of West Country dialects, like the
one of Cornwall, who were using the same *a'* that Shakespeare
knew, such that *he isn't* was *aw bain't*. People speaking such
dialects were common among the whites who migrated across
the Atlantic to work plantations in the Caribbean and there-
abouts starting in the 1600s. People speaking standard English and living cozy affluent lives in London tended to be the
ones who ran the plantation trade from their homes and of-
fices, with no inclination to relocate across the ocean to hot,
unfamiliar places.

Thus African slaves working in the first English plantation

colonies heard this *a'* version of *he*, and the first creole English they developed, whose Surinam variety was transplanted to Jamaica in the 1680s when that island was colonized, had not *he* or *'e* but *a*. "He loves" in the creole called Sranan in Surinam today is *A lobi*. Not *Hee lobi* or *Him lobi* but *A lobi*. This was a new language entirely, used more for black people to talk to one another than to talk with whites. It was as much African as English, and was not properly English at all. But it was stamped with things like Cornwall English pronouns.

But in Jamaica, over time this original creole was used alongside English itself so much that it became more like it. The result was today's Jamaican patois, straddling the line between dialect and separate language. An English speaker can learn to wrap their ear around Jamaican patois over time, and Jamaicans themselves tend to think of the patois as a kind of English. In contrast, to an English speaker the original creole would have been as impenetrable as Swedish, as Sranan is today to a modern English speaker.*

---

*The original creole's descendant languages, Sranan, Saramaccan, and Ndjuka, are still spoken in Surinam. There, the official language is Dutch: people use Dutch formally and one or more of the creoles casually. The creoles were born in the brief fifteen years or so that the English occupied the colony before it was given to the Dutch. They formed with (mostly) English words, and thus have not had English to

This didn't mean that the original creole vanished entirely in Jamaica, though. Some slaves in Jamaica luckily escaped plantation servitude and made new lives in the mountains. They spoke Jamaican patois, but worldwide people tend to have more than one way of speaking their own language, and these ex-slaves also still knew the original creole. They just came to use it differently than the people who first spoke it did. Just as "that one" once just meant "he" but is now used in a narrower way to convey a certain flavor, by the late twentieth century the old creole was now used in a narrower way, brought out only in ceremonies communing with ancestral figures.

Thus there is what these Jamaicans call the "deep" creole. And in these ceremonies, *he* and *she* are either *a* or "aw" (written as *o*). "He came from salt water" is *O kõ frã sali wata*; "He hit me" is *O naki mi*. Dialects like the one of Cornwall have been extinct for eons now, but these Jamaican men are using the same pronoun as Shakespeare's Claudio.

---

melt into since. Thus the creoles are in no sense varieties of Dutch, having developed on their own and stayed closer to their original state. They are versions neither of English nor Dutch but new languages entirely, which one must learn from the bottom up rather than adjust to. Sranan is the vernacular, as opposed to formal, lingua franca of Surinam; Saramaccan and Ndjuka are spoken in the interior by descendants of slaves who escaped plantations in the same way as the Jamaican ones did.

On with the Show, This Is It*

We have seen that English pronouns started as the elegant little trio of *he, heo,* and *hit.* But entropy meant that *heo* became *she* and *hit* lost its *h.* Thus the jagged little skyline of *he, she,* and *it,* and the object pronouns where the perfect *him, her, hit* is instead *him, her,* and *it.*

The casual reality has restored the tidiness in its way. The object pronouns as actually pronounced in casual speech are *'im, 'er,* and *it.* The apostrophes, making the first two seem somehow temporary or offsite, are a mere orthographic fashion: the reality is *im, er,* and *it.* Could be worse.

But the question is why *hit* should have lost its *h* and not *he,* and chance has a lot to do with it. There are versions of English where *he* is always *'e* or *'im*—this is especially common in creoles like Jamaican patois. And more to the point, an English dialect can last forever, or close to it, and keep *it* as *hit.* The Shetland Islands dialect is an example again, with *Hit wis a mercy* and *Hit fell wi' a dad*—I like that sentence for some reason; a *dad* is a lump!

---

*From the theme song of the grand old *Bugs Bunny Show* on late twentieth-century Saturday mornings.

But it has stayed *hit* in the United States as well, in earlier Southern English. For some reason this never got around as a stereotype, but it jumps out in, for example, Faulkner, such as in a 1939 short story, "Barn Burning": "He aims for me to lie, he thought, again with that frantic grief and despair. And I will have to do hit." And as with most (but not all) white Southern American English language traits, it was also common in older Black English. Zora Neale Hurston's characters often speak the authentic rural Black English she grew up hearing and later documented in fieldwork. It can be somewhat challenging to read, in part because of now foreign usages such as *hit* in this passage from *Jonah's Gourd Vine*: "Member now, you done started dis and it's got tuh be kep' up do hit'll turn back on yuh," which meant "it's got to be kept up or otherwise it will turn back on you."

It was, for a spell, defective. Something often missing in Shakespeare is the possessive form of *it*, *its*. This is because while Old English splits nouns into three genders, for some reason the possessive of *it* was *his* instead of the *its* we would expect, which only came along later out of a quiet sense that, well, it *should* be *its*! That took longer than we might think, such that Shakespeare was still using *his* with things.

It makes for odd little moments, such as in Polonius's famed speech to Laertes in *Hamlet* where he advises: "Give thy thoughts no tongue / Nor any unproportioned thought *his* act." That is, don't give vent to a thought you haven't considered carefully. But since when is thought a boy? This is something else we moderns ought be spared in real-time experience with Shakespeare's language, if you ask me.

While we're on *his*, it was also the reason we mark the possessive *s* with an apostrophe. In Old English, nouns "conjugated," so to speak (we actually term it *case marking*), in the way that we saw that German still does. For example, the word for *stone* was marked with suffixes for different cases, with different suffixes for plural versus singular:

	SINGULAR	PLURAL
STONE	stān	stānas
OF THE STONE	stānes	stāna
TO THE STONE	stāne	stānum

These case suffixes, in line with English's eternal quest to shed the unnecessary, dropped away over time, such that by Middle English the only one left was the *-s* one for the possessive, as in *stānes*. Neither in Old nor Middle English was this suffix marked with an apostrophe. Why would it be? Nothing was "missing."

By Middle and Early Modern English, then, there were

three ways to mark the possessive. The first two will be familiar; the third will look peculiar:

1. Toms book (with no apostrophe)
2. The book of Tom
3. Tom his book

The third one was once common, especially in casual
speech. Speech, though, is quick, and so, naturally, for "Tom
his book," people often said "Toms book." On paper, this was
written as "Tom's book," where the apostrophe marked a missing *his*. But since now the possessive ending -*s* and the *'s* that
was short for *his* sounded the same, it was easy to think that
when you were saying "Toms book," the first way, you were actually saying "Tom's book." It came to feel right, then, to always write the apostrophe with possessive *'s*.

After a while no one said "Tom his book" anymore, but the
apostrophe habit had settled in, despite no one thinking of it
as standing in for something lost. It became the useless but
hopelessly entrenched punctuational custom we are familiar
with, whereas in German the possessive -*s* ending is generally
not marked with an apostrophe (*Siegfrieds Buch*, "Siegfried's
book").

His is possibly responsible for possessive *'s* having even survived in English at all. It would have been perfectly normal, and perhaps even expected, that Old English would shed all the case markers. In an alternate-universe English, the possessive would be marked only with *of—the book of John—* or with brute juxtaposition, where context would indicate the meaning—*John book*. Black English allows exactly this, in fact, as do countless languages in indicating possession. The reason the old *-s* ending, and only that one, held on is quite likely because there happened to be the "Tom his book" version in competition, which, when contracted, happened to come out as "Tom's book" sounding just like "Toms book." That was an accidental resemblance: as always, amid all the rules and patterns that drive language change, serendipity always plays its hand. (As in, Laura Dern's!)

Why Not *It*?

In our times, as we get used to new uses of *they*, I suspect that more than a few of us wonder why our gender-neutral pronoun cannot be *it*, which, after all, is neither masculine nor feminine. I have more than once heard people stumbling when attempting to refer properly to a nonbinary person, bumbling briefly into *it* before chuckling and correcting it to *they*. To use *it* seems to make such sense, and yet as soon as it comes out of our mouths it instantly feels like a barbarity.

This is because the essence of *it* is more than having no gender. *It* also lacks personhood. The book sense of *it*, as in the one I have been presenting, is as merely one of a jolly lineup of possibilities where the implication is "either gendered or not":

But this misses something. *He* and *she* have personhood; *it* doesn't. To wit: in layman's terms, "*It* can't be a person." But in technical terms, *it* lacks *animacy*, while *he* and *she* have it. The feminine aspect of *she* is one type of something more basic about it, its animacy. This is why the name of the Addams family's cousin is funny.

The grammar book version at the top is handy but crude; the reality is at the bottom:

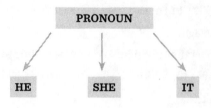

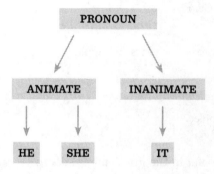

Animacy is one of those things that many languages observe in more obvious ways than English prefers to, such that to its speakers, no one like me would need to point it out. It's like how cuisines value things—Italian garlic and tomatoes, Thai shrimp paste and fish sauce, Ireland's lamb and potatoes, Scandinavians and those little red berries they put in everything. Some languages are all about animacy. Really,

Anglophony is a tad animacy-blind, as it were—that irritation with nuance again.

One learns that in Spanish *a* means *to*, but then grapples with sentences like "I kiss Carlos," where you have to say you kiss "to" him:

Beso a Carlos.
I kiss ? Charles.

Whereas you don't kiss "to" apples:

Beso   manzanas.
I kiss apples.

The use of *a* in the first sentence doesn't mean "to" anymore, just as *gonna* doesn't refer to going and *let's* doesn't refer to granting permission. It's a different word altogether, now a homonym of the *a* that means "to." It is now a piece of grammar, used because Charles is alive and apples aren't (not even farmers market ones with real flavor—I recommend the Stayman if you can find it). To wit, this *a* is what linguists call an animacy marker.

All languages have their ways of marking animacy, in one

corner or another. In Japanese, you learn early that *tachi* is the plural marker and think it's the same thing as our plural *-s*. But stick around and you learn that you only use it with what is often phrased as something like "people, children, pets." If you use *tachi* to try to say "books," it's a goofy mistake unless you're going for something like "booky-poos" or "these bad boys" that pretends they are kind of alive.* That is, *tachi* is a plural marker used only for animacy. Japanese prefers to show pluralness only with living things, figuring that beyond them, you probably know whether it's just one thing or more of them anyway, and that if you don't, you might as well guess. After all, how likely is it that context won't make it clear?

Languages differ on marking animacy even with their *it* words. In Russian, it feels easy to extend the *it* pronoun to nonbinary people. This is because the language assigns three meaningless genders just as Old English did, and in all three genders there are both living and nonliving things: masculine men but also masculine tables, feminine women but also feminine forks, neuter insects but also neuter windows. In a

---

*"These bad boys" is usually used with food, as in putting hot dogs on the grill. I'm trying to think of a context where you would refer to books that way, going into that creaky voice usually used when saying it. "Mrhhh… now let's get these bad boys into boxes!"

language in which an *it* can already be alive, it feels less numb and dismissive to use *it* to refer to a human. Our English *it* is kind of an inert clod in comparison.

But it wasn't always, and is not even always today, depending on where you look. Even a modern English variety can still summon its old spirit of marking inanimate things with genders, and far beyond calling ships and cars things like Betty. This happens, as may not surprise you at this point, in the Shetland Islands.

Tools and things about the weather are *he*. The world, the moon, fish, and some matters of time are *she*. Masses of stuff like grass, hay, and mold are just *it*. Imagine a hypothetical English, 2093 CE, descended partly from Shetland English and partly from modern American with its new *she* usage. The textbook, for some reason in the font style of British ones from the Edwardian period, would have it as:

The gender assignments of certain nouns must be carefully learnt:

MASCULINE	FEMININE	NEUTER
wrench	dress	grass
storm	hill	hay
hail	burrito	mold

English as a *normal* European language?! All well and good, but fantasy helps us little in a quest for a gender-neutral pronoun that occasions no controversy. In sillier moods, I wish we could smash *she*, *he*, and *it* together and just use *shit* as a gender-neutral pronoun.* But then, imagine not wanting to specify the gender of someone and saying, "Last summer I dated shit." Let's face it, this would push homonymy beyond what context could gracefully take care of.

However, a gender-neutral pronoun has emerged spontaneously closer to home than the Shetland Islands will feel to most of my readers: Baltimore, Maryland! Specifically, in the Black English of younger folk there. The new pronoun is, of all things, *yo*.

This is neither the *yo* as in *your* (*yo'sistah* for "your sister") nor the interjection *Yo!*, nor the version of this interjection used at the end of a sentence to solicit empathy and agreement (*Dem was some good times, yo!*). This *yo* is used in ways delightfully counterintuitive to an outsider. Someone watches a guy tucking in his shirt and says *Yo was tuckin' in his shirt!* Note: this referred not to some "you" tucking in his shirt, but

---

*Now you know why I titled the chapter with "S-he-it." As in the magnificent Isaiah Washington's trademark "Sheeee-it ... !" My father used to say it with gusto after he had had a few.

some "he"! *Yo is a clown* is a remark about someone else being a clown, not the "you" being spoken to. And this *yo* applies to women as well as men: *Yo handin' out papers* means "She is handing out papers," recorded when someone was referring to a female teacher.

It would appear that a new kind of grammaticalization happened. It started with the interjection *Yo!*, which is a call, very outwardly focused. This lends it a kind of third-person quality within a conversation, which is inherently about me and you talking. The call *Yo!*, being inherently about that which is not us right here, lent itself to a quiet reinterpretation: as a slangy way of referring directly to those who are neither I, we, nor you—to wit, he or she. This is a beautiful example of the Jeff Goldblum water droplet on the hand: you just never know what the pathway will be.

Giving Our Pronoun?

Any language is bedecked with fossils, things that once were living and sensible but now get dragged along just because. The *were-* in *werewolf* once meant "man." Take *namesake*, *keepsake*, and *forsake*, and try to figure out what *sake* means. Nothing, today—it's a fossil. Habits stick.

The tradition of specifying which pronouns we prefer for ourselves has entailed a bit of fossilization as well. In our times, civility means that we do not assume that all people want to be addressed as either he or she. Rather, people tell us that they would like to be called he/him, or she/her, they/them, or even she/they or he/they.

But there is a question as to why we give the object form as well as the subject form, or quite often these plus the possessive form: he/him/his.

After all, the object and possessive forms come "for nothing." To speak English is to know automatically when the form is *him* or *his* rather than *he*. And it would seem (1) an interesting idea but (2) vanishingly rare that anyone would wish to be called *she* as a subject but *him* as an object, or *he* as subject, *him* as object, but *their* in the possessive, and so on. "I knew he was tipsy when he tried to touch the tip of her nose and instead just fell on her butt." "She took a picture of theirself to send to his mother." "They broke his toe in the shower and was limping for a week." To embrace such sentences would be an eccentricity to say the least.

The reason for the he/him tradition is that with created gender-neutral pronouns like *ze* and *fae*, it is necessary to spell out what the object and possessive forms are. These forms were used more commonly before the new hegemony of *they*, and one could not know automatically that the object form of *ze* is *hir* (or *zir*) or that the object form of *fae* stays as *fae* (but the possessive is *faer*). Hence ze/hir, fae/fae, et cetera.

It was natural given this format to list *he/him/his* in the same way. One followed a certain rhythm, as it were. A pattern held on, in the same way as we keep saying *namesake* and *forsake* despite no longer actually using the suffix *-sake* with a sense of its meaning. This is how language works, always and forever.

But if we rolled the dice again, we would likely just give *she, he, he or they, she or they, they*. And it bears mentioning that we could do so with no harm to clarity.

We would seem to be inching into *they* territory. It was inevitable: pronouns have a way of not staying in their cages, and the one that has been least inclined to, for the best part of a thousand years, is *they* (*them/their?*). It would be impossible to write a book on pronouns where *they* did not start coming up before its own chapter. And now, the chapter *it*-self.

* 5 *

THEY WAS PLURAL

I	we
you	you
he, she, it	they

If *I* is a show of its own, *you* is overworked, and *we* can't really be bothered, *they* is a shape-shifter.

First moving house into a new word entirely like a hermit crab appropriating an old shell, then becoming both plural and singular at the same time, and finally sticking with it in the face of endless critique, *they* has always had its own way.

Recall that in Old English, the third-person pronouns, across singular and plural, had gotten a little oddly similar. It already throws us that *she* was this thing *heo*. *They*, though, was not some antique-sounding version of *they* like "theogh" but *hie*. And often *they* came in a different form—but it was *heo*, the same as the word for *she*! Kind of a mess.

This all means that while the words for *I* and *you* in Old English were different from what we know but relatable, the third-person pronouns, other than *he*, were utterly foreign to us:

I	ic	WE	we
YOU	þu	Y'ALL	ye
HE, SHE	he, heo	THEY	hie (or heo)

And so darned *alike*—all these little words that look like coughs. As always, languages can be tolerant of soundalikes— as we know now from how we torture little *you*—but there are times when the irritation of context overtakes the irritation of nuance.

Such as what may happen when *he* and *she* are *he* and *heo*, while *they* is *hie* and then *heo* again!

It Could Have Been "The Whites of *Heir* Eyes"

What to do? If you've read this far, you can guess. When your personal pronouns wear out, you reach for *that*, *this*, and *the*. Around the same time as English speakers started using the feminine *that*-word *seo* instead of *heo*, they started saying "those ones" for *them*. The word was *þa* and was the same in all three genders:

MASCULINE	FEMININE	NEUTER
se gafol	seo cuppe	þæt fyr
the fork	the cup	the fire
þa gafola	þa cuppan	þa fyr
the forks	the cups	the fires

After a while, because language always changes, *þa* became *they*. It had related forms that underwent the same kinds of changes. Old English was all about agreement, remember, and so it wasn't going to be satisfied with just one word *þa* meaning "those." Certainly just as now we have *he* as the subject and *him* as the object (well, supposedly!), in

Old English, if *those* was a subject it was *þa* ("Those are what I want") but if it was an object it was something different, *þam* ("I want those"). That *þam* became what we know as *them*.

There is another story that gets around. Those of you who are fans of ye olde historie of Englysch may be waiting for the idea that English yoinked *they, their,* and *them* directly from the Old Norse that Scandinavian Viking invaders spoke, rather than DIY-ing it with what was already in English itself as *þa, þam*, and also *þara,* which became *their*.

That account goes down easy, because Norse did stuff English up with at least a couple thousand words, of which several hundred are still part of the basic vocabulary of our language. When Judy Garland sang "Get Happy," any Viking "fans of Judy" looking down from above knew what she meant. Humble words like *egg, skirt, knife, ugly, window,* and *scare* are not Old English but Old Norse. On *skirt* English didn't even need it—there was already *shirt,* and the two versions of the same Proto-Germanic word gradually divided their territory with shirts above and skirts below. It was the same with ditches and dykes—the same but different: dykes up here, ditches down there. But it feels good, like a postprandial digestif, to top it off by supposing that even *they, their,* and *them* were Viking imports, especially since Old Norse's "they" pronouns were *þeir* for *they*, *þeira* for *their*, and *þeim* for *them*.

But despite that tempting resemblance, the whole idea has never quite made sense.

Languages just don't share pronouns much. It happens, on the margins here and there. But generally, pronouns are baked too deeply into the very DNA of how we talk to feel "right" used in another language. Languages sharing pronouns is like people sharing toothbrushes. Even if you aren't that uptight, just...nah. With a modest command of Spanish, for example, it is easy for an English speaker to get a sense of how odd it would be for Old English speakers to have started using Old Norse pronouns.

Imagine someone saying this utterly spontaneous, ordinary sentence:

"Goodness gracious! Guess who's handing out the milk? Them!"

Now, there are various parts of this sentence that we can imagine being replaced by Spanish, in a context where many people are bilingual in English and Spanish and thus naturally tending to mix the languages to an extent. Quite plausible would be:

"¡**Ay caramba!** Guess who's handing out the milk?
Them!"

Even replacing *milk* with *leche* could work if someone is being playful. A Kansas white friend of mine with no Spanish-speaking heritage has a cat named Leche and uses Spanish pet names with his friends (yes, I am Juan), and I can imagine him saying:

"¡Ay caramba! Guess who's handing out the **leche**?
Them!"

But. Subbing in the Spanish word for *handing out* sounds ridiculous even as wordplay:

"¡Ay caramba! Guess who's **repartir**-ing the milk?
Them!"

And then, to replace the pronoun *them* with *ellos* is so hopeless the speaker would seem a tad damaged in some way:

"¡Ay caramba! Guess who's handing out the milk?
¡Ellos!"

This is because languages borrow some things more easily than others. Separable items like *of course, however, then*, and *goodness gracious* have a way of jumping the fence. Nouns do it much more easily than verbs: *I don't have any dinero* is much more likely than *I don't tengo any money*.

When I was in college, I worked in the dining hall for a while, and one of the adult staffers was given to asking young male students whether they wanted to make extra money working on catering orders with him on the weekends. (I was never aware of anyone actually doing so.) His line was "Ya wanna work catering?" My roommate and I had a joke that there was a movie about him that was so popular it was shown in Germany where the title was *"Ya Wanna Arbeit Catering?"* (*work* in German is *arbeiten*).* I'm laughing as I write this forty years later; the thing worked on so many levels. One was how willfully dumb it would be for the one translated word to be the verb *work*. In the right context, the guy might possibly have started saying, "Ya wanna work Gastronomie?" But not "arbeit catering"!

Once you're arbeiting catering, or tengo-ing dinero, you're

---

*For those who have been so gracious as to have read one of my previous books, *Nine Nasty Words*, this is the man I described as a "brilliantined fellow with a pencil mustache" who was always saying "Everybody shits on me!"

on your way to creating a hybrid language. And this is also true of pronouns. "Nosotros decided to wear purple instead of white"—it's hopelessly implausible. Old English speakers were not implausible.

Their language, weird *heo*s and *hie*s and all, felt as perfect and personal to them as our modern English does to us. There would be no reason for them to start saying *ellos*, as it were, rather than *them*. The only thing that has made this seem likely is that Norse's *þeir* looks more like our modern *they* than Old English's *þa* does—although not that much. Plus, in terms of the rules of how sounds changed from Old English to now, we would expect *þa* to have become *tho* rather than *they*. These things are (relatively) regular across every word that has the sound. If the Old English word for *stone*, *stan*— pronounced "stahn"—didn't become pronounced "stain," then why did *tha* become *they* instead of *tho*?

But the thing is that Old and Middle English existed in legions of dialects. *They* first emerged in northern England, and up there, sound changes flowed in a different direction down Laura Dern's hand. Namely, words like *stan* became *stone* only down in the south. Modern research has shown that northward, words like *stan* became *stain*—that is, *þa* could become *they* in the same way, and then spread to the rest of England and beyond over time.

Finally, a smoking gun is one scribe translating the four Gospels into Old English in the 900s CE. He knows nothing of Old Norse, inking the English words under the lines of Latin in the original document (the beautiful Lindisfarne Gospels). He translates Latin's *they* words not into Old Norse versions, but good old Old English *þa* words. This is a precious *Archaeopteryx* document. In fossils we can see when a reptile becomes a bird—a toothed bird with a long tail that probably flew only so well. In the Lindisfarne Gospels we can see how English speakers got rid of weird *hie* and *heo* for *they*, sounding too much like the word *heo* for *she*, by dragging in the word for "those ones," *þa*, which would eventually be pronounced "they."

So, no hissing *heo* and no sharing toothbrushes. Fixing the Old English third person was all about making new uses of *this* and *that*—literally. But about as soon as *they* was nicely settled in, it started nosing out of its lane. Quite a few have never gotten over it.

What's Wrong with a Singular *They*?

There are times when we wish to refer to a singular person out of many, and also are not concerned with marking that person's gender. "With that door unlocked, every employee will think they can just go in there and grab a snack whenever they want to." The reference is singular—the mental image is of a single employee. But the use of *they* makes a kind of sense. It emerges from the fact that we are thinking both of one person grabbing those Cheez-Its and the fact that several people have been doing it.

Much of language marks things not explicitly said. This is the logic, for example, of the seemingly nonsensical and yet now ubiquitous *Yeah, no* meant as agreeing with someone. "Yeah, no—so many things work like that now." The *no* is not the usual one in a usage that for some reason doesn't make sense. One says *no* in such a case as a subconscious response to an implied denial, of which you and your interlocutor are both unspokenly aware. The 1.0 statement is that many things work like that now. The 2.0 aspect of it is that you are stating this for a reason: that many people do not know that things work like that now, and might even deny that they do. If you think about it, much of conversation is about asserting what is true in the face of many people's unawareness of it. "Yeah, no—the algorithms are designed to keep you addicted." "Yeah, no—one in five species of mammals are bats." *Yeah, no*, in its way, covers cognitive territory more thoroughly than only saying yes.

In "With that door unlocked, every employee will think they can just go in there and grab a snack whenever they want to," the *they* stems from the same kind of subconscious precision. We're thinking of several people while referring to the action of one of them, and hence, the drive to say *they*. And this usage, "singular *they*," came about long, long before *yeah, no*. It goes back to the Middle Ages, because of how strong, and natural, the impulse is to have a way of expressing a generic *one* while also thinking of this *one* as being one of many.

To make it maximally clear how deeply rooted in the very guts of English singular *they* is, we have to stop by Middle English for a bit, despite that it is different enough from our language as to seem like a wayward dialect of Swedish.

Geoffrey Chaucer is rarely accused of being slovenly with language, and in the Pardoner's tale in *The Canterbury Tales*, way back in the 1300s, he wrote:

And whoso fyndeth hym oute of suche blame
Thei wol come up and offre in goddis name

In other words:

And whoever finds himself out of such blame
They will come up and offer in God's name

The *whoever* is one person, with the third-person singular ending *-eth* (or later, our *-s*). And yet Chaucer, thinking of more than one person having this experience, refers to them as *they.**

Chaucer's frame of mind on *they* was normal, and writers in English have harbored it richly in his wake. I love this list from 1895 of ancient examples of singular *they* from celebrated writers:

Had the doctor been contented to take my dining tables, as *anybody* in *their* senses would have done. —AUSTEN.

If the part deserve any comment, every considering *Christian* will make it *themselves* as they go. —DEFOE.

Every person's happiness depends in part upon the respect *they* meet in the world. —PALEY.

**The Canterbury Tales* survives in many handwritten manuscripts, in many of which the scribe a century later "corrected" this *they* to *he*. What is significant is that some of these manuscripts, from the better part of a millennium back, nevertheless did have the singular *they*.

Every nation have *their* refinements. —STERNE.

Neither gave vent to *their* feelings in words.
—SCOTT.

Each of the nations acted according to *their* national
custom. —PALGRAVE.

The sun, which pleases *everybody* with it and with
themselves. —RUSKIN.

Urging *every one* within reach of your influence to be
neat, and giving *them* means of
being so. —RUSKIN.

Everybody will become of use in *their* own fittest
way. —RUSKIN.

Everybody said *they* thought it was the newest thing
there. —WENDELL PHILLIPS.

Struggling for life, *each* almost bursting *their* sinews
to force the other off. —PAULDING.

Whosoever hath any gold, let *them* break it off.
—BIBLE.

Nobody knows what it is to lose a friend, till *they* have lost him. —FIELDING.

Where she was gone, or what was become of her, *no one* could take upon *them* to say. —SHERIDAN.

I do not mean that I think *any one* to blame for taking due care of *their* health. —ADDISON.

This list was compiled by two serious people, likely steeped in William Blake and William Dean Howells, and voting for William Jennings Bryan—one of them was even named William himself—who thought of all these quotations as *errors*.

We would seem to be in the same territory as the idea that English speakers effortlessly handle endless grammatical complexities but stub a toe when saying "Billy and me went to the store." When the supposed confusion is so very common, the possibility looms that the confusion is among the complainants.

Always and forever, there have been people insisting that singular *they* is wrong because "*they* is plural." Which is indeed how it began. But things change. Sand is mountains. Mammals are fish. Or, sand *was* mountains and mammals *were* fish. Singular *they* is as natural a change as how sand and mammals have emerged. After all, if "*they* is plural," then we might have to insist that "*they* is *hie*," and there seem to be few takers there.

But if no one thinks *they* is *hie*, quite a few have thought it should be *he*.

As in, many of our grammar stewards have thought our sentence should be "With that door unlocked, every employee will think **he** can just go in there and grab a snack whenever **he** wants to." As it happens, the inaugural salute to that solution was from a woman, schoolteacher and author Ann Fisher, in 1745. "The Masculine Person answers to the general name, which comprehends both Male and Female; as, any Person who knows what he says," she noted.

This passage, however, is more factoid than history in the making. What truly imprinted the idea that "*they* is plural" is Lindley Murray's runaway hit English primer from 1794 onward, the first guide to "proper" English usage with universal impact. So universal that through the 1800s it was referred to generically as "Murray" the way today we refer to "Strunk and White," it was Murray from which generations of students and status-conscious bourgeoises learned that "Can anyone, on their entrance into the world, be fully secure that they not be deceived?" was an erroneous sentence, needing correction to "Can anyone, on **his** entrance into the world, be fully secure that **he** not be deceived?"

The overt masculinism of these prescriptions, alone, renders them obsolete. The idea of processing both men and women when hearing *he* is an absurdity, as we saw in chapter 2. However, too often we have been taught that the solution is just to include *she*. As a product of the final decades of the twentieth century, I was raised to suppose that the civilized new thing was to use *he or she*, and either alternate this with *she or he* or alternate between using *he* alone and *she* alone. Or in writing, to use the lovely and intuitive *he/she* or the unpronounceable *s/he*; I assume some have used *she/he*.

But none of this has ever worked gracefully. For one, amid the subconscious and rapid nature of casual speech, keeping track of whether one has said *he* or *she* often enough is essentially impossible. Casual speech is as resistant to narrow control as an electric guitar solo; a polite quantifiable balance between *he* and *she* could only be maintained via the deliberation of writing. Also, even if we are accustomed to processing *he* as (supposedly) generic, to hear *she* used in alternation certainly sounds ungeneric, signaling only women.

And then, *he or she* and *she or he* sound constructed, canned, and uncongenial in casual speech. Imagine using either while wearing a baseball glove or naked. And even in writing, they do half the job at best. Witness:

> Everybody likes chocolate, doesn't he or she?
> Everybody was very polite because he or she was on his or her best behavior.
> Everyone was delayed by the traffic jam, and so I was relieved when she or he arrived.

Yes, you can rephrase. But is there really a reason why we must? What is the problem—as in wrong, bad, backward, inexplicit—with *they* being both plural and singular, especially when even singular *they* has a resonance of its original plurality, just as singular *y'all* does? We use singular *they* within a mental frame of there being many potential people in reference, regardless of gender. To say "With that door unlocked, every employee will think **they** can just go in there and grab a snack whenever **they** want to" is to think of a sped-up feed from a surveillance camera of legions of employees grabbing those snacks from time to time—a plural kind of singular.

Tempting, maybe, is the idea that we should still keep pronouns in their pens as a kind of aesthetic choice. Even if we are capable of managing using *they* as singular, there could be room for arguing that we should not. We trim the lawn; we get the poodle haircuts; we keep a sachet in the closet (I actually don't!). Could we not keep our set of pronouns civilized and tidy, even if it qualifies as an artifice? After all, cat shows, manicures, and hair spray are artifices, and no one tells us to get over them (well, maybe hair spray, but for scientific rather than aesthetic reasons).

As a finicky person, I completely get why some might feel that way. But as a linguist, I simply cannot, because of how real languages work worldwide. Few will be more useful here than Dinka, one of the many languages spoken in Sudan.

If you ask a Dinka speaker how to say *spear*, as in to spear something, the answer is *ṯàr*. It's what you would see in a dictionary, the basic word. But if you want to use it in a sentence, with pronouns, then you can only use it with *you*. Otherwise there are completely different forms. In Dinka, you *ṯàr* but he *ṯὲɛr*. Funny thing, though: if you had asked the speaker how to say "pull the spear out," then that is *ṯὲɛr* as well. As for "I spear," that one is *ṯáar*. But then the issue of pulling the spear out is relevant again—in a different way. If you say you *want* *to* pull the spear out or *have to* pull the spear out, then you use the form that also happens to be used with *I, t̠ɑ́ar.**

Don't worry, I'll stop. But this kind of thing is endless in Dinka: forms can have two or three different meanings randomly and to a very large extent, you just have to know. What I laid out above means:

	BASIC	ALTERNATIVE
t̠ɑ́ar	I spear	(I want) to spear
t̠ɑ́r	you spear	just "to spear"
t̠ɛ̀ɛr	s/he spears	to pull the spear out

And notice that the alternate meanings have no connection to the meanings of first, second, and third person. Plus, I have given you just a sliver: there is much, much more going on in Dinka. Plus it differs verb by verb. It's rather awesome.

Now imagine some eighteenth-century bookworm in a periwig about to die of yellow fever, deciding that it's wrong for Dinka to use *t̠ɑ̀r* for "you spear" because "Oh no: *t̠ɑ̀r* is already

---

*The mark under the *t* means that it is pronounced on the back of the teeth, the accent marks indicate tone, and the two dots mean that the word is pronounced in a slightly breathy way.

the basic dictionary form. Alas, how *inimical* to Sense is such a Limitation to the Second Person." Unthinkable. We assume that Dinka does fine the way it is, and we are correct. Why would anyone try to fix something that works?

"*They* is plural" is the same mistake, regardless of the smarts or accolades of whoever insists. A word in any language can be many things, with no threat to clarity or even nuance. Context, as you can see from Dinka, is mighty, as it is in all languages, including English. No one hearing singular *they* has ever asked, "Do you mean one person rather than two???" unless they were trying to make a point. And that point is deep-sixed by Dinka—as well as the entire history of Middle and Modern English.

If You Try Sometimes, You Can Get What You Need

The resistance to singular *they* has eased considerably in the twenty-first century. It's high time, because it never made actual sense. What made the difference was the increasing visibility of people resisting the gender binary. Media people, generally tilting progressive in their politics, were in a bind. They were minted in a tradition of observing traditional norms of grammar in deference to their consumers but also dedicated to acknowledging the legitimacy of people wanting to be neither *he* nor *she*. The latter concern won out.

A key moment was Bill Walsh, *Washington Post* copy editor, writing in 2015: "Allowing *they* for a gender-nonconforming person is a no-brainer. And once we've done that, why not allow it for the most awkward of those *he* or *she* situations?" I have yet to address matters of identity. But Walsh's point was that if we allow singular persons to be referred to as *they* in the new way that occasions controversy, then obviously we must let go of this aging pox on singular *they* referring to people grabbing KIND bars from an office canteen.

But even amid progress, conservativity hangs on. The *AP Stylebook* and the *Chicago Manual of Style*, as I write, approve of singular *they* only if it serves to explicitly cloak gender, as in for people who would prefer to be addressed as *they*. Under that allowance, "With that door unlocked, every employee will think they can just go in there and grab a snack whenever they want to" is still wrong because there is no particular quest to avoid specifying whether men or women are involved. This position is in fact antique, held for instance by those grammarians named William in 1895, who also only sanctioned it when used as an avoidance strategy on gender.

As I write, the *Oxford English Dictionary* and *Merriam-Webster's* have shed hoary harrumphings and simply accepted singular *they* without the gender caveat. All indications are that august bodies in resistance will follow in their footsteps before long. The lesson, though, is that historical change is driven, in disconsolately large part, by serendipity.

Analogy: the civil rights victories in America of the 1960s were not driven conclusively by widespread understanding of the reality of racism. What helped transform America was that television could broadcast racist horrors from Birmingham, Selma, and beyond worldwide, during a cold war when America's leaders found it newly and conclusively awkward to be revealed as racist to a globe watching.

In the same way, the new acceptance of singular *they* has not been driven by a critical mass coming to understand that there was nothing wrong with it grammatically. Rather, a more explicitly gender-neutral *they* was recruited by a newly visible segment of the population whose acceptance had, blissfully, become a sign of moral enlightenment. It felt natural to bring old-school singular *they* along for the ride.

But as it has turned out, that segment has needed more than just old-school singular *they* as in "Tell each one they can come in." They need "Jocelyn paints their nails themselves."

When *They* Really Does Mean Just One

The most challenging new development in pronoun usage in the history of the English language is the use of *they* in reference to a specific person.

Grand old singular *they* was *non*specific in its reference. One was referring not to any individual, but to a human of vague description who mentally could be either male or female. This is different from someone wishing to be personally referred to as *they* rather than *he* or *she*.

    A. Where's Tyler?

    B. They just left.

This, folks, is new. This usage became widespread in the 2010s, with the American Dialect Society designating *they* as the Word of the Year in 2015 followed by *Merriam-Webster's* in 2019. The custom arising in that decade of asking people to "give their pronouns" was motivated in large part by the option of this new usage of *they*.

It throws many people. The old singular *they* was controversial enough, but largely on paper. Few people, even the most educated, have ever felt much shame in using singular *they* in conversation. Moreover, as I have noted, even if felt to be "singular," the old singular *they* has always felt tacitly right because its broader reference actually is plural.

The new *they* really does refer to only one person, with no plural reference even implied. Plus one must adjust to this novelty in one's casual speech. Then also, the request to be called *they* entails the courtesy that one complies, such that to slip and use *he* or *she* instead can be considered a gaffe. Beyond a certain age, one gets used to using the new *they* amid a certain sense of insecurity, of the kind you feel in venturing a sentence in a foreign language.

And it's not only in speech. The new *they* can be challenging to read, even with some of the most careful editing in the business designed to make prose as easily processible as possible. One venue committed to exquisite editing, quintessentially, is *The New Yorker*. Their profile of literary scholar Judith Butler referred to the scholar as *they* according to Butler's preference, and the result was (1) deferential, (2) modern, and (3) sometimes confusing.

A part of the article read:

> *The general secretary of the Central Council of Jews in Germany decried the decision to give the award, named for a philosopher of Jewish descent who fled the Nazis, to*

a "well-known hater of Israel." A demonstration was or-
ganized. Butler, a prominent critic of Zionism, responded
by citing their education in a Jewish ethical tradition,
which compelled them to speak in the face of injustice.

A reader would be pardoned for wondering whether *their*
referred to the aforementioned Central Council of Jews. One
gleans that it did not, and moves on:

Their academic work on gender from the nineteen-
nineties, albeit in distorted form, has incited recurrent
waves of fury.

Wait, whose? Academic work by which people? Oh—it's
the new *they*; so, just Judith Butler's.

From Eastern Europe to South America, right-wing
groups have portrayed Butler as not merely one of the
founders of "gender theory" but a founder of "gender"
itself—gender framed as the elevation of trans and gay
rights and the undermining of the traditional family. In
2017, while travelling in Brazil, where they had helped
organize a conference on democracy, Butler was met by
protesters holding placards depicting them with devil

horns. They burned a puppet bearing a witch's hat, a pink
bra,...

Wait—I'm used to thinking of *they* as meaning Butler. But here, okay, context furnishes that the *they* is people other than the scholar. Whew, but I'm on board.

... and a photograph of Butler's face—a "gender monster,"
Butler called it. At the airport, a fight broke out when a
protester tried to attack.

Butler and a bystander intervened.

Still, that evening in Paris, Butler did not flinch or pull
away. They responded, in French, "How am I threatening
your children?"

But exactly who responded in French? Especially as French is not Butler's native language, and few would spontaneously imagine Butler speaking it? Was it bystanders who responded in French? Bodyguards, as mentioned before? Or just Butler? I guess it makes sense that it was actually Butler.

This last reference to "they" especially challenges the reader, with how rapid reading is. As I write, I am in the middle of a tome whose author is given to referring to two or three *he*s in a sentence and then in the following one, making a reference to *he* that requires the reader to backtrack and decide which "he" makes the most sense. This is the result of sloppy editing, but if the best *The New Yorker* could do was the aforementioned passages, then the new *they* will apparently require a degree of backtracking. First-world problems, indeed—but still unideal.

Novelty, then, is not the only reason people can get itchy about the new *they*. And besides causing some ambiguity, it feels imposed, like a command. *You* creeping from the plural into the singular happened largely below the radar, bemoaned only by Quakers and the occasional pedant long after the horse was out of the barn. The reader likely doesn't know that *obnoxious* originally meant "subject to harm," with its meaning "noxious" happening over time. But the new *they* happened rather suddenly, a new social requirement that, to many, must have felt like it flashed into existence somewhere between when *The Office* concluded and Donald Trump announced he was running for president. I recall a doughty, erudite gentleman of a certain age and beyond, a respected scholar of language even, a tad Uncle Vernon in the Harry Potter series although quite nice, forcefully insisting in 2018 "I'm not doing it!," clearly affronted by a sense that he was being told to do something or go stand in the corner. But at the end of the day, changes in our culture are such that we need a gender-neutral pronoun in English. We need to join the Chinese and the Japanese and the Finns on this. It's going to feel new, it's going to feel imposed, and it's also going to feel a little ambiguous—because we have to use *they*. And that's because the alternative of a brand-new gender-neutral specific pronoun will almost certainly never get off the ground.

A Created Pronoun—No Matter How Clever— Will Never Catch On

Perhaps the most popular one has been *ze*; by my lights the most clever have been *hesh*—get it? *He* plus *she*?—and *per* (short for *person*). All of these coinages are diligent propositions by concerned citizens of language, civility, and progress. However, it is hard to imagine how they could truly prevail, short of a catastrophic societal reset that for some reason allowed that all children were raised hearing little but the new pronoun and incorporated it as their normal.

This is because pronouns are used so frequently, so below the level of consciousness, and correspond to categories so fundamental to human experience that they are all deeply resistant to change by fiat. *Homeless person* would have sounded willfully peculiar to someone in 1930, but Anglophone society easily adjusted to calls to eliminate terms like *bum*, *tramp*, and *street person* in the 1980s. This is because people without housing are, while an urgent issue, not something most people think and talk about around the clock. With a little practice, we easily peel the old label off and affix a new one. Getting Americans to use *Asian* and *African American* was no major challenge for the same kind of reason.

Terms that transcend gender can take longer to settle in, because of how prominent and all-pervasive the gender binary can seem. Progress happens, to be sure: *chairperson* and *spouse* are now ordinary. However, *wife, husband,* and *chairman* thrive alongside, whereas very few are talking of tramps, Orientals, and Negroes these days. Also, *actor* and *hero* for women have only gotten so far.

However, they have gotten *somewhere*, and this is because these labels such as *chairperson* and *spouse, homeless person* and *African American*, only come up so often. Pronouns, in contrast, are at the very foundation of human expression at all times. Full words are the windshield wipers and the headlights—things you turn on now and then. *He* and *she* are the accelerator and the brake pedal—what you are working down below, all the time, without thinking. The new *they* has to work so hard, in both referring to gender and being the change-resistant thing that a pronoun is.

Yet having a gender-neutral specific pronoun beckons strongly today, and the fact that so many languages have always had one as part of ordinary language makes the prospect even more tantalizing. But it's one thing to have a gender-neutral specific pronoun that was being used before the invention of agriculture, and another to advertise one today as a new invention. Goodness, humans like their pronouns the way they are, and a useful indication of this is in Nepal (stay with me!) in a language called Kusunda, spoken by but one person as I write, Kamala Khatri Sen.

Kusunda—actually a name assigned by outsiders; the people call themselves the Gemyehak ("tiger, king of the forest")—is one of the Basques of its region. Basque of France and Spain is related to none of the languages around it, or any other in the world. Kusunda is not a relative of any language anywhere near it. Except: way southeast of India, out in the Indian Ocean, is a chain of islands called the Andamans. A baker's dozen of indigenous languages have been spoken there, quite unrelated to any in India, or in Myanmar to their east. One of them is called Juwoi. Its speakers have no relationship to, much less awareness of, the Kusunda way up in Nepal, about as far away from them as Vermont is from Florida.

Archaeology and patterns of human migration suggest that Andaman Islanders reached the islands from the mainland about sixty thousand years ago, which means that Kusunda and Juwoi have been spoken by separate peoples, developing utterly independently of one another, for at least that long and likely longer. To get a sense of how different languages are after that much time, English and Russian are thought to have had a common ancestor eight thousand years ago at most, and likely less. And after that amount of time, in English one would say:

> One afternoon, I met the most beautiful woman in the whole world.

But in Russian, its relative, descended from the same language as English is, one would say:

> Odnazhdy dnjom ja vstretil samuju krasivuju zhensh-chinu v vsem mire.

Not a thing matches.

And yet, behold Kusunda and Juwoi, which might as well be spoken in Atlanta and Port-au-Prince, respectively, in terms of distance:

	KUSUNDA	JUWOI
I	chi	tui
YOU	nu	ngui
HE, SHE	kite	gida

For *I*, Kusunda has *chi* and Juwoi has *tui*. The *t* and the *ch* are variations on the same thing: *t* often drifts into becoming *ch*, as we know from how commonly people pronounce *tree* as "chree."

The similarity between Kusunda's *nu* and Juwoi's *ngui* for *you* is obvious.

Then, for *he/she*, *kite* and *gida* may not look much alike on the page, but notice that the *k* and the *g* sounds are the same but different. Then try the same thing with *t* and *d*. There is a reason the luscious meat is called *cappicola* in Standard Italian but *gabagul* in Sicilian: *g* is what often happens to the *k* sound of cappicola's *c* after a while. On *t* and *d*, think about how "Forget about it" comes out in classic New Yorkese as "Fuhgeddaboudit." Kusunda's *kite* is cappicola and "Forget about it"; Juwoi's *gida* is gabagul and "Fuhgeddaboudit."

kite	cappicola	Forget about it.
gida	gabagul	Fuhgeddaboudit!

In short, *kite* and *gida* are variations on the same word.

Now, accidents happen, especially when words are short. There are only so many possible sequences of a consonant and a vowel. One might therefore dismiss these similarities as chance.

But first of all, with these particular similarities, really?

And second, the way the two languages say *my* and *your* makes that dismissal much less plausible.

	KUSUNDA	JUWOI		KUSUNDA	JUWOI
I	chi	tui	MY	chi-yi	tii-ye
YOU	nu	ngui	YOUR	ni-yi	ngii-ye
HE, SHE	kite	gida			

To make it *my* and *your*, both languages add a suffix. That's important because there are lots of ways a language might make *I* or *you* possessive. A suffix, as in Kusunda and Juwoi, is one way. A prefix, though, is another. You might also change the vowel as in *my* versus *me*, or even use some completely different word. It isn't only that Kusunda and Juwoi both use a suffix—that alone would not suggest that they were related—but the suffix is practically the same one in the two languages. What are the chances this is an accident?

And there is no way that these resemblances happened

from speakers of the languages coming together and imitating each other. This is no "¡Ay caramba! Guess who's handing out the milk? ¡Ellos!," despite that Kusunda and Juwoi, even if in contact, would have been no more likely to trade pronouns like this than English and Spanish. The Kusunda were hunter-gatherers tucked away in the forests of Nepal; the Juwoi were way off down in the Andamans, distant via all of India and then a goodly swatch of ocean. There had been no contacts of any kind between speakers of these languages.

With all due respect to the rigorous caution of some evaluators, I feel confident in assuming that the pronouns in these two languages reveal them as related. Sixty-thousand-plus years ago, a group of people split from another group. Descendants of some of the ones who split off now speak Juwoi in the Andamans; descendants (or as I write, descendant) of some of the ones who were split *from* now speak Kusunda in Nepal. Today, the pronouns reveal the common origin. This is the only possible explanation for how closely they match.

In all that time, entire ice ages have come and gone. All but a few of the two languages' words (beyond pronouns) have become unalike to a degree vastly beyond English's and Russian's. But the pronouns have sat tight, remaining similar enough to indicate a relationship utterly lost to their speakers, historical documentation, and even specific archaeological evidence.

The lesson from Juwoi about English pronouns? *People really, really like their pronouns to say the same.*

And not just around the Indian Ocean. In the Proto-Indo-European language of roughly six thousand years ago, which birthed almost every language in Europe and a great many in Iran and India, the pronouns were about like this:

I	ego^h	**WE**	we-i
YOU	tu	**Y'ALL**	yus
HE/SHE	he/se^h	**THEY**	te^h

I is something that *ego* became, as we have seen.* The *we* and *y'all* words speak for themselves. For the singular *you* word *tu*, remember that originally English had *thou*. *Tu* to *thou* is A to B. The third-person pronouns were words for *this*, *that*, *these*, and *those*, which English either took on directly from the source (in the case of *he*) or got by subbing them in from what they had become in English later (*she*, *they*).

---

*The ^{h} stands for something we may never know precisely but was some kind of throaty sound that we can know was there based on detective-style reasoning. That reasoning was confirmed by the digging up in Turkey of ancient clay tablets in the Indo-European language Hittite, unknown until then, which actually had throaty sounds in words exactly where ghostly suggestions in living Indo-European languages show they must have once been. Intrigued? It's called historical linguistics.

The point is clear: English pronouns today are only modestly changed from the ones people were using in Ukraine several millennia ago. To wit: *People really, really like their pronouns to stay the same.*

Making Our Way with *They*

This, then, is why we must accustom ourselves to using *they* in a new way rather than making up a new pronoun, as plausible and even fun as that may seem. Using a new pronoun would be like trying not to ever touch anything with your middle fingers. It just couldn't be.

So we must work with what we already have. *He* and *she* are beside the point. *I*, *we*, and *you* would be insane. *It*, having never referred to persons, would sound like a slur. This leaves *they*. At least it was already being used in the singular anyway. But even if it hadn't been, the simple fact is that *they* is all there is.

Plus, *they* has already been there, serving gender-neutrally in sentences like "Anyone can tell when they're tired." There are now attempts to create and normalize gender-neutral pronouns in other languages. In most if not all the cases, the new pronoun is used more in LGBTQ+ and educated circles than elsewhere. But if anything makes these gender-neutral pronouns catch on even further, it will be because there was no preexisting singular *they* already serving something close to the purpose.

There are now versions of *hesh* across Europe in particular, such as French's *iel* (*il* + *elle*), Swedish's *hen* (*hon* + *han*), and German's *xier*, pronounced "zeer," combining German's "she," *sie* (pronounced "zee"), and its "he" word, *er*. In Spanish, a blend of *él* and *ella* would just yield *ella* again, and thus *elle*—"ay-yay"—where the *-e* ending is intended as a compromise between the masculine *o* and feminine *a*. In Portuguese, where the same problem would occur with *ele* and *ela*, the new pronoun is the lovely *elu*.* Polish is closely related to Russian, but using the *it* word for people has not caught on there as much as in Russia. Combining *on* ("he") and *ona* ("she") would have the same problem as in Spanish and Portuguese, and thus *onu*.

Other languages are newly recruiting forms of *they* for the job. This is especially common in the Balkans, with Greek, Bulgarian, and Romanian, but also with Irish. Elsewhere are quirkier solutions. In Vietnamese, especially in emigrant

---

* *Little Women* would have been better if there had been a fifth sister, Elu.

communities, one gender-neutral pronoun combines *chị* ("sister") and *anh* ("brother") into *chanh*, a word that happens to mean "lemon"! Even Esperanto, the world's most successful artificial language, commonly engaged by language-heads like me as curious teens, has gotten with the times. *He* is *li* and *she* is *ši* ("shee"), and the new(ish) gender-neutral pronoun is *ri*. And nobody really knows why—it just feels right, apparently!

Meanwhile here in English, it is natural to feel that *they* is being worked almost strangely hard. In the crosslinguistic sense, it is. To encounter a language with as few personal pronouns as Berik in Papua (the western half of the island New Guinea) is to quietly wonder how people avoid confusion. On singular versus plural, there is only a distinction in the first person, between *I* and *we*. Otherwise, Berik stretches *you* the way English does, but furthermore has but one word for *he*, *she*, and *they* (and *it*):

	I		*we*
	ai		ne
you, y'all		i	
he, she, they		je	

And yet, with the new *they*, English is becoming quite a bit like Berik in this regard. Under an idea that Anglophone societies might stop labeling the gender binary with pronouns at all, our grid would be:

	I		we
		you	
		they	

And today's reality is close enough to Berik's itself:*

	I		we
		you	
	he, she	they	

But the main thing is that Berik speakers do not think of their pronouns as a problem, and instead likely wonder why speakers of other languages need so many more of them.

As such, we can be sure that our newly streamlined pronoun grid is compatible with the basic needs of human cognition.

---

*Berik's lightness on pronouns must not be taken as evidence that it is in any way a "simple" language otherwise. The word *gweranswetna* means "I placed three objects or fewer in a high place near to you." *Terbefe* means "You will give a large object to a man in the dark." And these are perfectly normal words, not idioms. An English speaker could spend a lifetime failing to master Berik; the pronouns would be just a welcome break.

And no, it is not that Berik speakers get along with a single third-person pronoun because they live in small villages, more people know one another, and you can always just point to people you are talking about. The very purpose of *he*, *she*, and *they* is to be able to refer to people beyond yourself and your interlocutor, and as often as not, those people are not present to be pointed to. The villages aren't *that* small! Besides, this would leave unanswered why English manages without a *y'all*. As we have seen, the eclipse of *thou* happened in cities, not villages.

Our job is to manage. There are two important indicators that we can.

One is that quite a few people are already doing so. A survey of several hundred people in 2019 showed that the new *they* was accepted, and often used, by most subjects under thirty-five, was more often dismissed by subjects over fifty-five, and elicited mixed feelings among people between thirty-five and fifty-five. Nonbinary and trans people were especially likely to approve of and use the new *they*.

In other words, rejecting *they* is a mark of the "olds." One often observes people in their teens and twenties (and even tweens) using the new *they* quite effortlessly these days. My daughters were doing so in reference to two people of our acquaintance at the tender ages of six and nine, correcting me as I flubbed despite my best intentions.

The second indication we can handle the new *they* is that it is a foundational experience as an English speaker to master something else unnatural: always using *I* as a subject pronoun.

If you're reading this, you've likely mastered keeping subject and object pronouns separate, even to the point of not having to think about it. But if even after chapter 1 you are still of the opinion that "Billy and me went" is wrong because you don't say "Me went," saying "Billy and I" is always and forever an add-on, a filter, a break from intuition. Without asserting that I am somehow representative of all English speakers, I will readily admit that my primal impulse is to say "Him and me were the ones they saw going over there." And I do say things like that in casual, unrecorded moments. "He and I were the ones they saw going over there" is, to me, like putting on dress shoes. It is no more my true, spontaneous impulse than it is for a kid to write a thank-you note.

If all of us have mastered this rule that no child understands, a rule you can't even speak English without breaking ("Who did that?" "Me!"), then certainly we can master a new way of using *they* that feels unfamiliar. "Jocelyn and she were the first ones in the room" is no more or less natural than "Jocelyn paints their nails themselves." It's just that we're less accustomed to it.

We can do this. It will be easier the younger we are, but

still. There was a time when casual command of the rewind / play / fast-forward / pause format marked one as with the times (my mother never picked it up). There was a time when eating sushi was considered kind of swanky, with people of a certain age thinking of eating raw fish—*raw fish!!*—as unthinkable (someone had to literally stuff it into my mouth when I was twenty-two [1988] to show me how good it was). In the 1980s, many show tune fans in their fifties and older disliked the work of Stephen Sondheim, despite that it took the genre to a new level and is now endlessly revived and even made into movies.

There comes a time in many lives when people are less interested in acquired tastes, added skills, new practices. Using the new *they* will be one of those things for some. But this makes it neither an error nor a joke. There is all indication, from where I sit at this writing, that the new *they* is the future.

Walking Against the Wind

The story of *they* in English starts with an attempt to keep *he*, *she*, and *they* from falling together, and yet today many are engaged in seeking that they now do just that. This is a beautiful illustration of how culture can influence language change.

The link between culture and language is fitful, to be sure. It undersells the multifariousness of language change to depict it as driven solely, or even mainly, by what its speakers are like and what they do over time. Pronouns generally change very little despite seismic cultural change happening around them. Meanwhile, the reason in many languages one can say something like "I poked him while him slept" is usually because of a gradual reinterpretation of what starts out as "He was poked *by me* while he slept," none of the change connected with culture in the slightest.

If anything, when culture changes language, and this quickly, it's hot news. The new *they* represents an unusually direct and powerful synergy between culture and how we put words together, against which resistance will create mere turbulence. The historical record is rather thin of societal changes occurring rapidly, embraced by most stewards of public culture, but eventually going extinct because older and fussier people weren't on board.

The new *they* should be, I would venture, a matter of etiquette. A fervent few will reject the etiquette, proudly wearing tube socks in the summer or (and??) insisting on using aerosol hair spray, hoping the new imposition is a passing fashion and willing to deal with the friction in the meantime. Most will observe the etiquette to the best of their abilities. But, it is hoped that those under a certain age will understand that those abilities will be less than stellar, at least for a while. They should understand that we're gonna slip up here and there given how quickly this has happened. My sense is that most of this cohort do understand that having to master a new pronominal usage after several decades of life is difficult, with mental faculties, no matter how sharp, no longer as fluid as they were in our teens and twenties. I am pretty sure I represent people of a certain age in saying that using the new *they* feels at first like learning to drive on the wrong side of the road. Learnable, but goodness, one must attend closely at first.

But to not adjust puts one at the risk of becoming what a later age looks upon, justifiably, in derision. In 1935, Virgil Thomson thought himself acerbically insightful in writing:

> *The material is straight from the melting pot. At best it is a piquant but highly unsavory stirring-up together of Israel, Africa and the Gaelic Isles . . . I do not like fake folklore, nor bittersweet harmony, nor six-part choruses, nor fidgety accompaniments, nor gefilte fish orchestration.*

Tartly put, but no one wanting to be taken seriously today would venture this take on the magnificent opera *Porgy and Bess.*

Young people know that rock has the beat of sexual inter-
course. And in what does progress culminate? A pubescent
child whose body throbs with orgiastic rhythms; whose
feelings are made articulate in hymns to the joys of onan-
ism or the killing of parents; whose ambition is to win
fame and wealth in imitating the drag-queen who makes
the music.

Brilliant expression of a view shared by many back in the day, but Allan Bloom's take on rock and roll began aging badly at the moment of its publication in 1987.

The spices in it are bad, the vinegar is a seething mass of
rottenness, full of animalculae, and the poor little inno-
cent cucumber, or other vegetable, if it had very little
"character" in the beginning, must now fall into the ranks
of the "totally depraved."

Topic: the pickle, by an educated American taken seriously in 1886.

I suspect that resistance to the new *they* risks looking in the future like Thomson, Bloom, and Dr. Susanna Way Dodds do now, and that the healthiest strategy will be to just enjoy the ride.

What they wants?

I find it impossible to resist doing something linguists are not supposed to do.

Namely, I harbor, and must share, *advice* on how we use an aspect of the language. I propose a way to make the new *they* easier to accept and use.

As I have indicated in this book, spoken language does not usually respond meaningfully to prescriptions. But the new *they* is new territory, and thus there may be more room for flexibility than usual. My prescription will also make things tidier. Moreover, social forces ever more influential in modern American English could serve as wind under its wings.

———————

People often ask whether the new *they* is to be used with verbs marked *-s* or not. "Is it 'they wants' or 'they want'?" people ask, with a tone implying that *they wants* would be faintly ridiculous. I always answer that the new *they* is used with an unsuffixed verb, just as *they* has always been, despite referring to a singular person.

But this is not the way it has to be. Actually, it might be more intuitive to people if the new *they* actually *were* used with the *-s* ending. As such, the grid would be:

I want	we want
you want	y'all want
she/he/they wants	they want

Why, precisely, not?

To the extent that the new *they* does create ambiguity as to whether one or more people are in question, the *-s* would neatly solve that problem. Into the nineteenth century, English speakers attempted a similar cleanup in the use of *was* and *were* with *you*. The language was on its way to using *was* with *you* in the singular, instead of carrying over *were* from the plural. "You, George, were the only one there" sounded a little off; certainly, if "I was" and "he was," then "You, George, was the only one there." "Where, sir, was you on the night of the 22d of December, 1799?" a lawyer asked during that murder trial in 1800 mentioned in chapter 2—and note that as a lawyer he was an educated man steeped in the written word.

The only reason this cleaned-up usage of *was* never settled in for good was blackboard grammarians insisting that "*You* takes *were*," as if time never passes and change is always bad. They must be seen in view of those who have insisted that "*They* is plural" in the same frame of mind. But in that light, "They wants to do their nails themselves" would be less susceptible to confusion than "They want to do their nails themselves." This could be the time we allow logic to prevail.

One thing inspiring my suggestion is that the new *they* is already used this way in Black English. In the dialect, present-tense conjugation can be the opposite of the standard English rule, such that -*s* is used with all pronouns but *he*, *she*, and *it*:

STANDARD	BLACK ENGLISH
I want	I wants
you want	you wants
she/he wants	she/he want
we want	we wants
y'all want	y'all wants
they want	they wants

This means that a Black English speaker might say, using the new *they* in reference to a single person:

Mrs. McDonald, I don't know why they gots a problem with me. I mean, I done taught them every damn thang they knows! Quiet as it's kept, or better yet, loud as it is, I betcha they wants my job!*

---

*Thank you, Demarttice Tunstall!

It would seem that our times are especially well poised for the acceptance of using *-s* with the new *they*. This is because of the general "browning" of American culture since the 1990s.

It has included the mainstreaming of hip-hop, which has had much to do with infusing casual American speech with a dusting of Black Englishness. Generations of non-black Americans have now grown up with the slang, grammar, and cadences of Black English in their ear day in and day out through this music, to a degree that was unknown beyond occasional outlier kids before the 1990s.

And the new reality extends beyond music. A useful example is the speech patterns of comedian Aziz Ansari, who is of South Asian descent but whose voice could easily be mistaken as that of a black man if only experienced through audio. Crucially, in our times, this aspect of Ansari occasions no comment, as opposed to in, say, 1979 when he would have been processed as "the Indian guy who talks like a black guy."

Black English is much more familiar to the mainstream American ear than it once was, to the point that one could designate it, with only modest exaggeration, as America's youth lingua franca. White guys casually call each other "bruh." A gay white character on the sitcom *Only Murders in the Building* warns that "Nina will cut a bitch!" using black female slang in a way that real-life versions of him often actually do. I recently heard a white radio announcer, of mostly mainstream dialect, saying that someone was a major fan of Taylor Swift and "Ain't nothin' wrong with that!"—a way of putting it that would have been alien to his equivalent on this kind of show before the twenty-first century. To extend the concept of language to gesture, non-black girls of all extractions use the side-to-side slide of the neck to indicate indignation in a way that once was solely a black female gesture. Hip-hop is gleefully played at very white weddings with no one batting an eye. Black English "flavor" now seasons American life to an extent that seems trivial only to those who weren't alive and mature in the 1980s or earlier, when American English and its gesticulations were much whiter.

In this light and even beyond, the line between formal and informal speech is much thinner than it once was in American language, and we might consider allowing *they wants* to cross it. Authenticity, anyone?

———

To be sure, *they wants* may nevertheless sound somewhat odd at first. But then, part of why the new *they* in general seems odd to many is in its verb being *s*-less when referring to a single person. To use it with *-s* could make it seem somewhat more, to create a word I need here, *wieldy* to the novice.

We need only a little imagination. How we allocate linguistic forms in terms of formality and correctness can differ strikingly from era to era. John and Abigail Adams regularly used *you was* in their letters to each other. *Ain't* also once had a different feel to middle-class and even affluent people. The men of the 1870s in Anthony Trollope's *The Way We Live Now* are men whose wealth has sunk below the level of their titles, but they are still "gentlemen," with property and "plate" and Houses in Town and such. Yet they use *ain't* as just another contraction, more or less as acceptable in civilized speech as *isn't* and *wasn't*. Felix Carbury—played in the miniseries version by *Succession*'s Tom, Matthew Macfadyen, to give you a sense of his type—says:

> *But what is the use of his coming to me? I know what he has got to say just as if it were said. It's all very well preaching sermons to good people, but nothing ever was got by preaching to people who **ain't** good.*

Lord Nidderdale—note, *Lord*; these are not Dickensian people of the alleyways or Alfred Doolittles—tosses off:

*But then she don't want me, and I ain't quite sure that I
want her. Where the devil would a fellow find himself if
the money wasn't all there?*

Note also his *don't* instead of *doesn't*. Trollope was depicting, casually, what English folk processed as civilized speech at the time, which was only 150 years ago, not 1,500. And, this was no British peculiarity. Around the same time in America, the *Little Women* characters were using *ain't* in a way just as unexpected to the modern eye or ear. "You'll be sorry for this, Jo March, see if you ain't!" says Amy, while at another point Meg says—and at a formal party—"Take care my skirt don't trip you up." Note also that Meg and especially Amy are the daintier of the sisters; the *ain't*s hardly come only from tomboyish Jo. Again, I am just one person, but to my ear, *they wants* feels negotiably okay, and I often find myself using the *-s* with the new *they* and then correcting myself. If it were decreed that from now on singular *they* were to be used with *-s*, I would get used to it and even kind of enjoy it like a new cocktail.

I doubt I am alone.

* Afterword *

WHAT'S YOURN IS MINE

At first, there was only *mine*, with no *my*. *Mine* was used not only in a sentence like "That's mine," but also as what we now use *my* for. One said "mine book," "mine apple." For the record, at this time the word was pronounced "meen"— "meen book." (Or actually, "meen *boke*"!) This is the kind of thing that would have left us only able to understand Chaucer in flashes.

But words that get a lot of wear get shorter. After a while, one said just "mee book," "mee cat," "mee tree" in rapid speech. And after a while, even when not so rapid.

Then, three things happened.

First, for a spell, you used "mee" before consonants but still "meen" before vowels, because the *n* was easier to pronounce before them. "Mee tree" but "meen apple" that fell from it. "Mee dog" but "meen elephant" (to the extent that they referred to them much). That may seem a little wrinkle that I maybe find more interesting than you do! But actually it led to a quiet mishearing that created some warm corners of English. If "mee" and "meen" coexist, you might start hearing things.

You love Ed, and often say "My Ed"—but we're still in Middle English and so what you actually say is "Meen Ed." But think of a toddler hearing a family name wrong, with their cute version, then catching on. "Gammy" for "Granny," or a guy named "Brud" because that was his little brother's rendition of "brother" (or at least that's what a guy told me once; he was kind of odd). Well, Medieval Junior might hear you as saying not "Meen Ed," but using that other form "mee" and saying: "Mee Ned." That is, "My Ned." Junior is calling Ed "Ned"—and in adoring imitation, soon everyone else is too. Granny, Gammy; Ed, Ned.

Here is why Ned is the nickname for Ed, which otherwise makes no sense. When have you ever given someone a nickname by tacking an *n* before it—"My sweet N-Julia"? "I just love me that little N-Stuart!" Nah—the only way this could happen is subconscious accident. It also explains Nellie for

Ellen, Nan for Anne, and the now obsolete Nabby for Abby, which was a nickname for Abigail Adams, among others.

Second came English's Great Vowel Shift starting in the 1400s. Part of this meant that in words with the "ee" sound, it changed to "aye." Where once one—such as Chaucer—said "niece wheat reese," one now said "nice white rice." For the same reason, what was once "mee niece wheat reese" became "my nice white rice." This is why we say "migh" instead of "mee."

Third was something that did *not* happen. The Great Vowel Shift is often presented as if applying to all of English, but it was actually a story focused on southern England, where the standard dialect happened to form. Things went differently elsewhere. As an analogy, think of how the history of the 1920s in the United States is often told as if what happened in New York defined everything, except for some gangsters shooting people in Chicago and President Harding dying for some reason in San Francisco. The Great Vowel Shift was great indeed, but it was just one story, and it would have been strange if "ee" became "aye" uniformly in every English dialect in what would become the United Kingdom. That change was, in the grand scheme of things, a matter of chance.

As such, especially in heavily used words, where old habits can die hard, the "ee" could hold on. Donald Trump once recalled how, at the Battle of Gettysburg, Robert E. Lee called to his troops "Never fight uphill, me boys!!" Or not—Lee was neither Irish nor a pirate from Cornwall, and the utter absurdity of Trump's story and the imitation were sublime (Lee never advised downhill maneuvers, nor apparently did anyone else). But Trump was, quite vaguely, onto something: there are English dialects where one still says "me boys," which is simply a medieval holdout pronunciation.

One hair out of place about *mine*, though, is why isn't it *mys*, when this is the pattern with the other possessive pronouns:

mine	ours
yours	yours
his, hers, its	theirs

The funny thing is that our natural question is upside-down in terms of what the original situation was. It's *yours* and *ours* that should be like *mine*.

In English, as originally spoken, the properly dressed possessive pronoun ended in an *n*. The old movie with Lucille Ball and Henry Fonda combining families (years before *The Brady Bunch*) would "authentically" have been *Yourn, Mine, and*

Ourn. Today we associate forms like *yourn* with Appalachian dialect. But in fact, the original Middle English situation was:

mine	ourn
thine	yourn
his, hern	theirn

Note that even the possessive form of *thou* had been *thine*, matching *mine* sweetly instead of being *thouse*.

His was the odd one out, in not being *hin*. But it was also the one that felt like it made a certain sense, in that the *-s* ending was the same one that English uses for the possessive in general: Ed's book, Robert E. Lee's accent, Ryan's hope, Papa's little dividend, he's—*his*—book. Thus the final *-s* on *his* started spreading to the other possessive pronouns. It felt right.

In their language, people both retain oddities out of habit and seek pattern. When literacy has yet to become the default, with no reign of pedants insisting that the way the language looks on the page is the way it must stay, humans of normal mental vigor and predilection do their jobs. This is where English speakers created *yours*, *ours*, et cetera. Only *mine* held out, with the *I/me* zone having its way of holding on to things, as we have seen. "I Gotta Be Me," as the old song had it.

Yourn and *ourn* are the kind of thing that has encouraged the grand old notion that Appalachian English preserves "Elizabethan English." But actually, the Appalachian forms emerged through taking English back to the past. Instead of people going from *his* and turning *yourn* into *yours*, in Appalachia, people went from *mine* and turned *yours* "back" into *yourn*! But of course they had no way of knowing it was "back," or sideways, or underwater. Each generation speaking any variety of any language operates within its own local reality. The rich morphings of English in Appalachia happened with no cognizance of what had happened almost a thousand years ago across the ocean in the Dark Ages.

Changes today happen at the end of a never-ending process of transformation, from a bygone stage where one addressed someone as *thou*, two someones as *inc*, and more someones than that as *ye*, while the word for *she* was *heo* and the word for *they* was *hie*. Go further back than that and people were likely saying "This, me" where we would say "I," and using the word *that* for *he* and *she* and *those* for *they*.

People using these earlier forms of our language thought their pronouns were normal. It's harder for us to always feel that way, because any new development contrasts starkly with the original form shining black and permanent in print. Then it stirs the pot faster when the change is connected to social factors, such as when *thou* comes to sound like a putdown, or calls arise requiring the use of *they* to refer to one person.

That's just it: pronoun trouble is due to the fact that pronouns are what we are. But in the end, pronouns are the latest stage in something always changing, just as we are as people. Our job is to adjust to the inevitable awkwardness of change, in our pronouns as in ourselves. After all, as a look through a photo album always confirms, spectating how we got from there to here, even if there were some awkward phases, is a lot of fun. The beat never stops, and few of us wish it would.

Acknowledgments

This book was, in truth, a fast and easy birth, written in a burst of inspiration that I owe fundamentally to my agent, Dan Conaway, who is so good at zeroing in on topics that interest (1) the reading public and (2) me. Tracy Behar at Penguin Random House was excellent at making me realize that even in mid- (late mid-?) career as a public-facing linguist, I could still learn a thing or two about getting out of my own head and writing it clear. For remediating assorted ignorances of mine, thanks are due to Bjarke Ballisager, Andrew Gerle, and my former students Emily Gul, Levi Cohen, and Demarttice Tunstall; to fellow language scholar (and in-law of a sort!) Ilan Stavans; and to linguists Marianne Hundt, Mikael Parkvall,

ACKNOWLEDGMENTS

Peter Bakker, Lane Greene, Oksana Laleko, and Geoffrey Pullum (who was especially invaluable in directing me, after going to the trouble of surveying colleagues, to sources actually addressing the notorious but understudied pox on *me* used as a subject pronoun).

NOTES

The internet allows a reconception of the purpose of reference sections like this. I here provide sources only for the more idiosyncratic references in the text, for which guidance on where to search would be useful.

Chapter One: The "Your Highness" of *I*-ness

16 **"Everything would be cut and trimmed out":** Freiburg Corpus of English Dialects (Mid/SAL_039.txt:191).

17 **many sources of evidence make it clear that in the nineteenth century, this usage of *am* was common:** Specialists have traditionally thought otherwise, but I am taking the liberty of pushing the envelope a bit because recent research using hitherto unmined sources has made a case for this early usage of *am*—which I, for one, find compelling—that I am not sure said specialists have had

occasion to fully engage. I refer to: Me, "Revisiting Invariant *Am* in Early African-American Vernacular English," *American Speech* 95, no. 4 (November 2020): 379–407.

17   **a recording in 1940:** Irene Williams, on the Works Progress Administration Slave Narrative Collection, "Interview (Monologue) with Irene Williams and Choir, Rome, Mississippi," 1940, Library of Congress, https://tile.loc.gov/storage-services/service /afc/afc1940003/afc1940003_afs04016/afc1940003_afs040 16a.pdf.

23   **Here is how this relates to why *I* and *me* look so unalike:** Linguist Glen Gordon presents this hypothesis in the fashion closest to what I am translating here (check his blog); Merritt Ruhlen's idea was the broader one based on the Nostratic superfamily.

30   **in Old English and Middle English:** From F. Th. Visser, *An Historical Syntax of the English Language*, Part One (Leiden, the Netherlands: E. J. Brill, 1963), 90, 94.

32   **Parry Gwynne:** Parry Gwynne, *A Word to the Wise: Hints on Current Improprieties of Expression in Writing and Speaking* (London: Griffith & Farran, 1879), 16–17.

37   **one nineteenth-century grammarian:** John Mulligan, *Exposition of the Grammatical Structure of the English Language* (New York: D. Appleton, 1853), 504.

47   **Differences among the Germanic languages:** Thank you to Peter Bakker, Mikael Parkvall, Bjarke Ballisager, and Lane Greene.

49   **one John Mulligan:** This is the same man as the one cited in the note for page 37.

52   **The take-home point:** For handy debunking of the pox on *Billy and me* with some arguments I have not included for concision, I

recommend Rodney Huddleston and Geoffrey Pullum, *The Cambridge Grammar of the English Language* (Cambridge, UK: Cambridge University Press, 2002), 8–10.

Chapter Two: Poor Little *You*

59   **The situation was a little more involved:** The eternal classic description of how formality was handled with pronouns in medieval Europe and beyond is the invaluable and lucid Robert Brown and Albert Gilman, "The Pronouns of Power and Solidarity" of 1960. I hardly need specify a printed source it has appeared in; it has been endlessly reprinted and is now readily available at the press of a button.

65   **But instead, by the end of the 1600s:** A chronicle of the eclipse of *thou* must be drawn from many sources, but my favorite survey of the lay of the land on this and much else is Lynda Mugglestone, ed., *The Oxford History of English* (Oxford, UK: Oxford University Press, 2013). Relevant for this book's purposes are the fifth, sixth, and seventh chapters, with the latter, Terttu Nevalainen's "Mapping Change in Tudor English," especially useful.

76   **a drive to shed unnecessary baggage:** I describe this shedding process in more detail in *Our Magnificent Bastard Tongue: The Untold History of English* (New York: Gotham, 2008).

79   **"high-density versus low-density networks":** The classic article is James Milroy and Lesley Milroy, "Belfast: Change and Variation in an Urban Vernacular," in *Sociolinguistic Patterns in British English*, ed. Peter Trudgill (London: E. Arnold, 1978), 19–36.

82   ***Youse* was likely an import from Ireland:** A nice go-to on *youse* as well as the basics of *y'all* is Susan Wright, "'Ah'm Going for to

Give Youse a Story Today': Remarks on Second-Person Plural Pronouns in Englishes," in *Taming the Vernacular: From Standard Dialect to Written Standard Language*, ed. Jenny Cheshire and Dieter Stein (New York: Longman, 1997), 170–84.

84 **non-Southerners don't get the idea of singular *y'all* out of nowhere:** A widely consulted article that nicely lays out the evidence, including from sources before it (from which I get the quotes from the store clerk), is Gina Richardson, "Can *Y'all* Function as a Singular Pronoun in Southern Dialect?," *American Speech* 59, no. 1 (Spring 1984): 51–59. Richardson is a little more gimlet-eyed than I would be that anyone is *ever* addressed eye to eye with *y'all*, but I doubt she would disagree with anything I add, and her article is a fine case of what is necessary to actually nail the reality of things like this down.

91 **too many studies have shown:** One of them is Megan M. Miller and Lori E. James, "Is the Generic Pronoun *He* Still Comprehended as Excluding Women?," *American Journal of Psychology* 122, no. 4 (Winter 2009): 483–96.

Chapter Three: *We* Persisted

102 **the English that developed on Pitcairn Island:** The best source is Peter Mühlhäusler, *Pitkern-Norf'k: The Language of Pitcairn Island and Norfolk Island* (Berlin: De Gruyter Mouton, 2020).

115 **Pennebaker:** James Pennebaker, *The Secret Life of Pronouns* (New York: Bloomsbury, 2011), 175–76.

115 **the pronoun as a hugger:** For those who really want to follow the research on this, I learned much from Lenka Bičanová and Václav Blažek, "Indo-European Personal Pronouns: Limits of

Their Internal Reconstruction," *Linguistica Brunensia* 62, no. 1 (2014): 29–55.

Chapter Four: *S-He-It* Happens

127 **"Hoo's a bit set up":** Elizabeth Gaskell, *North and South* (New York: Harper & Brothers, 1855), chapter 8.

131 **If the English of the Shetland Islands:** The handiest source is Peter Sundkvist, *The Shetland Dialect* (New York: Routledge, 2020).

133 **this use of *she* has moved to a wider range of things:** My students Emily Gul and Levi Cohen made me aware of this (thanks, you two, for sharing with me what you knew I would find neat) with later invaluable reinforcement by Andrew Gerle, who also referred to the New York production of the musical *Chicago*, running now in New York since about 1872, as "She's tired."

135 ***Bloom County*:** Berkeley Breathed, *Bloom County*, December 3, 1986.

140 **the "deep" creole:** I am describing what is called by its discoverer Maroon Spirit Language. Consult Kenneth Bilby, "How the 'Older Heads' Talk: A Jamaican Maroon Spirit Possession Language and Its Relationship to the Creoles of Suriname and Sierra Leone," *Nieuwe West Indische Gids* 57 (1983): 37–88. The Jamaicans who used it had been speaking it as an everyday language until the 1920s. A study on the current situation is Audene Henry's 2023 PhD dissertation at the University of the West Indies, Mona, "The Languages of the Moore Town Maroons: A Linguistic Reconstruction and Sociolinguistic Analysis of the Language Lifecycle in an Oral Ritual Culture."

151 **The new pronoun is, of all things, *yo*:** First announced in Elaine Stotko and Margaret Troyer, "A New Gender-Neutral Pronoun in Baltimore, Maryland: A Preliminary Study," *American Speech* 82, no. 3 (2007): 262–79.

Chapter Five: *They* Was Plural

160 **¡Ay caramba!:** Thanks to Ilan Stavans for translating my sentence into good Spanish. The *¡Ay caramba!*, though, is mine.

163 **Finally, a smoking gun:** Invaluably convincing on this topic, after decades of propositions in its direction, is Marcelle Cole, "A Native Origin for Present-Day English *They, Their, Them*," *Diachronica* 35 (2018): 165–209.

168 **two serious people:** William Malone Baskervill and James Witt Sewell, *An English Grammar* (New York: American Book Company, 1895).

170 **I was raised:** George Jochnowitz, "Everybody Likes Pizza, Doesn't He or She?," *American Speech* 57, no. 3 (Autumn 1982): 198–203.

173 **endless in Dinka:** Data from Torben Andersen, "Vowel Quality Alternation in Dinka Verb Derivation: The Agar Variety," *Journal of African Languages and Linguistics* 38, no. 1 (1993): 1–50.

186 **For *I*, Kusunda has:** Paul Whitehouse, Timothy Usher, Merritt Ruhlen, and William S.-Y. Wang, "Kusunda: An Indo-Pacific Language in Nepal," *Proceedings of the National Academy of Sciences* 101, no. 15 (March 31, 2004): 5692–95.

189 **the pronouns were about like this:** There are always competing reconstructions of Proto-Indo-European. I am using that of Andrew L. Sihler, *New Comparative Grammar of Greek and Latin* (New York: Oxford University Press, 1995).

192 **as few personal pronouns as Berik:** Peter Westrum, "A Grammatical Sketch of Berik," *Irian: Bulletin of Irian Jaya* 16 (1988): 133–81.

194 **A survey of several hundred people:** Kirby Conrod, "Pronouns Raising and Emerging" (PhD dissertation, University of Washington, 2019).

199 **Allan Bloom:** *The Closing of the American Mind* (New York: Simon & Schuster, 1987).

199 **the pickle:** Susanna Way Dodds, *Health in the Household; Or, Hygienic Cookery* (New York: Fowler & Wells, 1886), 72.

ABOUT THE AUTHOR

John McWhorter teaches linguistics at Columbia University. Other books he has written include *The Power of Babel*; *Our Magnificent Bastard Tongue*; *The Language Hoax*; *Words on the Move*; *Talking Back, Talking Black*; *Nine Nasty Words*; and *Woke Racism*. He hosts the *Lexicon Valley* language podcast, has authored six audiovisual sets on language for Wondrium (the Great Courses), and has written weekly for *The New York Times* since 2021.